Other Works by Farley Dunn

A Journey Through 2 Timothy
The Beatitudes: Finding the Hand of God in Our Lives
Finding God Through Acronyms, Vol. 1-3
God and Discipleship for the Modern Christian, Vol. 1-6
God Desires Repentance From His Children, Vol. 1-2
God Desires Worship From His People, Vol. 1-2
God Is Faith in Our Despair, Vol. 1-5
God Is Hope in Our Darkness
God Is Salvation for a Lost World, Vol. 1-4
God Offers His Kingdom to All, Vol. 1-3
God Renews Our Relationships with Others, Vol. 1-3
God Uses Evangelism to Reach the World, Vol. 1-2
God Wraps Our Family in Love, Vol. 1-2
Power Confessions, Vol. 1-4
Power Quotes, Vol. 1-4
Relentless Love: How God's Unshakable Devotion Can Change Everything
The Thirteen Days of Christmas: A New Look at an Old Song
Understanding Paul's Epistle to the Colossians

Unending Grace

Embracing the Power of
God's Forgiveness

*Break the Chains of Guilt,
Discover Lasting Peace, and
Walk in the Freedom of Divine
Mercy*

Unending Grace

Embracing the Power of God's Forgiveness

——— *Farley Dunn* ———

UNENDING GRACE

By Farley Dunn

1st ed.

Subtitle: Embracing the Power of God's Forgiveness

Unless otherwise noted, Scriptures are taken from the NEW INTERNATIONAL VERSION (NIV): Scripture taken from THE HOLY BIBLE, NEW INTERNATIONAL VERSION ®. Copyright© 1973, 1978, 1984, 2011 by Biblica, Inc.™. Used by permission of Zondervan.

This book and its contents are wholly the creation and intellectual property of Farley Dunn.

This book may not be reproduced in whole or in part, by electronic process or any other means, without written permission of the author.

ISBN: 978-1-957173-52-8

Copyright © 2026 by Farley Dunn

All Rights Reserved

Contents

Introduction i

The Heart of Forgiveness 1

The Weight We Carry 22

Washed Clean 46

The Gift You Must Receive 67

The Freedom to Forgive 88

Forgiven for a Purpose 109

The Journey Continues 129

Introduction

Forgiveness.

It's central to the Christian faith. Forgiveness is the core around which the salvation story revolves. Remove forgiveness from the narrative, and all the rest falls apart.

The Old Testament prophecies about the coming of the Christ … gone!

The Old Covenant giving way to the New Covenant established by Jesus … out the door!

The cruel and unrelenting agony of Jesus' death on the cross at the hands of the Roman overlords … no point!

You see, forgiveness is crucial to our walk as believers, followers of the Christ, and adherents to the Christian faith. In this book, I hope to share a new understanding of the depths of God's forgiveness, the price Jesus paid on the cross, and why we can confidently let him carry the weight of our sins.

We don't have to earn it. It is a gift. Grace is not a graduated series of actions that draws us closer and closer to a divine state. We believe on Jesus, we ask for his forgiveness, and he *willingly offers it to us without regard to our social standing, pocketbook, or history.*

We are loved, we are forgiven, and we are desired. We need to accept God's forgiveness and live in it daily.

God's grace—his forgiveness—is waiting on you. Step into it today!

— I —

The Heart of Forgiveness

God's Unfailing Love for You

But God demonstrates His own love for us in this: While we were still sinners, Christ died for us.

— Romans 5:8 —

What is your test for love?

What do you require of people before you open yourself to them and let them inside your sphere of safety?

When older children are adopted and enter a new home, no matter how loving, they must grapple with the knowledge that they were first abandoned. Even if their parents died, even if they knew it was coming, the abandonment feels the same. The loss is primal and comes with the question: "How could they leave me?"

The next question is: "Will you leave me, too?" and they begin to challenge their new parents to "prove" their love and commitment. They have a need to experience their adoptive parents' unfailing love, to become confident that no matter how badly they behave, they will be forgiven and loved once more.

We are that child. When we accept salvation, we are adopted into the family of God. We are the one battering against his loving nature until he proves he will continue to love us no matter what.

Loving Because We Are Loved

We love because He first loved us.

— 1 John 4:19 —

Creation, the beginning of everything. With the touch of God's hand and the sound of his voice, the planets appear out of the vibrating superstrings that lie at the core of all matter. In the resonance of God's spoken word, matter comes into being, with light and dark, day and night appearing for the first time.

Psalm 139:1 reveals the connection between creation and humanity. "You have searched me, Lord, and you know me." Even before the act of creation, God knew we would one day be born. He intentionally spoke the world into existence for us to experience and enjoy.

When mankind—always mankind—made a mess of things, God's heartstrings were tugged, and in his love, he sent his Son to reconnect to us through his saving grace. We—mankind—had fumbled the ball, but God wanted us in his family anyway. Jesus became his message of forgiveness and love.

The Bible—God's written love letter to humanity—is our guide to God's character. John 10:10 reveals God's desire for his creation. "I have come that they may have life, and have it to the full." He desires us to enjoy a rich and satisfying life. Our well-being is firmly entrenched into the plan of God.

Why does God reach out to us over and over? Even when we fall on our face once again, he kneels beside us, lifts our face, looks into our eyes, and says, "I understand. Let me help you to your feet once more." He isn't an assembly-line God who rubber-stamps us when we come to the altar, then cries, "Next! Keep the line moving!" His love and forgiveness aren't a one-and-done experience. He desires an ongoing relationship with us, and he wants us to desire a relationship with him.

How do we know God wants to be in a relationship with us? First, he could have spoken the world into existence and then left us to our own designs. He could have peered down from his throne and mused, "They are sure making a mess down there. I hope they get it figured out one day."

No, instead he worked through the prophets, protected his people, and sent his Son to help guide humanity back to him. His initial act of creation was only the start. Jesus' sacrifice on the cross ignited the spark of reconnection, and today he continues to love us, provide for us, and guide us through the morass of pitfalls that is the human condition.

Let's return to our verse for a moment. As warm

and cozy as this verse is, it's the second part I want to look at. The first part tells us, "God demonstrates his own love for us." Okay, that's easy. If I get a new puppy, just having it is enough to arouse a level of love. I want to give it attention, to pick it up, to snuggle with it. It's so cute that I can't help but want it in my life.

Then it wets the floor. Or it chews on the new rug. It digs at the bedspread until it shreds the fabric.

Now how easy is that puppy to love? When I take it for a walk, and it tugs and pulls, and I trip and tear a hole in my new jacket ... I must prioritize my frustration with my feelings of how much I love the puppy. I must decide that while I don't like the mess the puppy creates, I do love the puppy, and it's worth my effort to clean up after it, to repair the bedspread, and to wear the tear in my jacket with pride.

That's how God feels about us. He forgives us even before we make a mess on the floor. The second part of this verse says, "While we were still sinners, Christ died for us." God is so in love with us that when we chew the new rug, he says, "I love the rug, but I love you more. Let's try again." When we tug and pull at our leash, and we create mayhem around us, God doesn't kick us out the door. He doesn't say, "I gave you a chance, and this is the last straw!" Instead, he helps us sort things out, puts everyone back on their feet, and says, "There, all better? Let's see if we can improve next time."

God loves us, he loves us, he loves us, even before we were born, even before time began. He loves us, and when we stumble, he's already forgiven us, even when we have trouble forgiving ourselves.

The Father's Open Arms

But while he was still a long way off, his father saw him and was filled with compassion.

— Luke 15:20 —

For those who grew up in the church, the Parable of the Prodigal Son is one we've heard in Sunday school, had acted out on storyboards in children's church, and seen portrayed at summer camps. It's a story of the human tendency to break away from expectations, to find our own path, and to establish our desire for independence, even when it hurts those who love us most. It also reminds us of the importance of never letting loose of our love, of the value of repentance, and how self-righteousness can destroy our connection to others.

This story is especially meaningful to Christians as it showcases our relationship to God. Even when we choose to go astray, he always stands with his arms wide, desiring our return, and gifting us with the finest he has to offer. That's God's unconditional love, a love that never wavers, even when we stray from the path he has plotted out and revealed to us. It's never too late to return to God. We've never gone so far that he will not accept us back. We are his creation, the ones he looks upon with joy and excitement, craving a renewal of our relationship with him.

Repentance.

He desires it at every turn. It's why he tugs at our heartstrings, places reminders in our path, and when we choose to see him for who he is, opens his arms and welcomes us into his fellowship once more. This showcases his forgiveness and grace, his willingness to forgive those who realize their wrongdoing and choose to turn from it. The son in our story asks his father for a place in his household as a servant, and the father offers him the best robe in the household. That's what God desires to offer us when we return to him. He doesn't desire a lengthy apology or that we demean ourselves through physical debasement or emotional humiliation. He finds joy when we simply return to him. In the story, when the father sees the son in the distance, he is so excited that he throws a party. His joy in reconciliation is evident, and through his joy, we see his love played out in his reunion with the son he thought was lost to him forever.

The prodigal son's brother, however, is a different story. He's stayed home, worked for his father, and been the dutiful son that his father must have hoped for. However, he's done it out of an expectation that he would receive more from his father than his brother. He felt entitled, even underappreciated, and because of that, he failed to connect with his father's joy on his brother's return. He missed out on the joy of the party because he felt the excitement should have been showered on him.

What made the difference between the two brothers? Why was his father's response to each different? One brother complained out of entitlement.

The other pleaded out of humility. He was willing to be a servant in his father's house rather than return to his position as a son ... and that broke his father's heart. His humility, his acknowledgment of his personal failings, and his willingness to accept the lowest of jobs ignited his father's grace to shower him with what he no longer deserved.

The prodigal son, at the beginning of the story, was determined to find his own way. He asked for his full inheritance and squandered it on lavish living. He journeyed away from the path his father had mapped out for him, and through his bad choices, he fell into hardship that threatened to swallow him whole. It's through seeking the guidance of God that we remain connected to him. It's in recognizing that we have failed that we can find our way back to him and have him fulfill his promise of restoration in our life. It's when we are far from God that we can most clearly see his light shining in the darkness. It's when the world has gone dark around us that his beacon of hope is at its most brilliant. It is through God's unwavering patience, love, and desire to reignite his relationship with us that we are called to him and welcomed back into his arms.

Grace Greater than Guilt

Where sin increased, grace increased all the more.

— Romans 5:20 —

Grace is transformative.

This means that it doesn't matter where we start, it matters where we are headed. In the Word, in Matthew 13:31-32, Jesus gives us the example of a mustard seed. It's the tiniest of all seeds, a mere speck when you hold it in your hand. With only a puff of air, it can escape and be lost.

However, plant a mustard seed, and it will grow and grow until it towers over us, providing shade for protection, wood for fuel, and fruit for consumption. You can process the seeds for oil for cooking and sometimes medicinal purposes, and the leaves are excellent for flavoring pickles, salads, and other dishes.

When planted, the mustard plant can serve as a cover crop to suppress weeds and control some pests.

It also sends down deep roots that loosen soil and enable the absorption of water and nutrients. They also release substances to counteract some soil-borne pests and diseases.

In some areas of the world, the oil is used to fuel lamps or as topical treatments during cold weather.

In essence, the tiny mustard seed transforms from something that is hardly of importance to something valuable, even life-changing in many instances. If we discount the mustard seed, which in the natural we'd easily overlook, we've missed an opportunity to grow something great out of what seems like nothing at all.

That's how grace grows to cover every sin. It's not rules and restrictions that get us to heaven. It's not attending church three times a week, saying a set number of prayers, or how much we drop in the offering plate. Galatians 3:19-24 says those things are placeholders to guide humanity until true grace can be offered through the person of Jesus and his sacrifice on the cross. "[19] Why, then, was the law given at all? It was added because of transgressions until the Seed to whom the promise referred had come. ... [24] So the law was our guardian until Christ came that we might be justified by faith."

The New Testament continues with this theme in I Timothy 1:14, Ephesians 2:8-9, and John 1:16-17. We read that grace is found in abundance through our faith in Jesus. When we struggle under the burden of many sins, we find equal relief to the weight of our sins. We don't have to "work off" our sins, or so-called "clear the slate" before we are worthy of God's love. Grace comes to us when we choose to believe on the Lord, for it is an unqualified gift from the Father above.

The Law, which came through Moses, was a guideline, a manual to keep mankind from going off the rails. It was a safety net until something stronger could be put in place. In the early 20th century, the Golden Gate Strait in San Francisco was an impossible barrier to travel. To even think about getting from one side to another was a heart-stopping, death-defying undertaking. The only option was to travel down the peninsula and back up the East Bay, a distance of sixty miles and possibly several hours. While the bridge was constructed, giant safety nets were erected underneath the superstructure as it rose above the strait, not as a passageway from one side to the other, but to keep workers safe if they fell from their stations. It was a dangerous undertaking. Of the thousands who participated in the bridge's construction through ten contractors, nineteen fell and were saved, and another eleven were lost.

Not everyone was saved under the Law. Some were still lost. Under grace, as revealed by the truth given to us during the ministry of Jesus, God's grace is extended to everyone, no matter their background, history of wrongdoing, or cultural identity. Jesus is the ultimate example of the mustard seed, for the truth he lived grew to shade the hearts of people the world over from the effects of sin and, through his redemptive grace, we flavor the world with the love of the Father.

You Are Not Too Far Gone

Though your sins are like scarlet, they shall be as white as snow.

— Isaiah 1:18 —

How far is too far for God to bring us back from the brink? For the Lord to step in and transform our lives from disaster to delightful? For the Savior to wipe our slate clean and create in us a new and pure self? What terrible things do we have to do, how badly do we have to live, how inconsiderate do we need to be for God to wash his hands of us and tell us we are no longer welcome in his family?

Yelling at our parents?

Refusing to support God's work?

Prowling the bars on the weekend?

Can we come back from these severe breaches of God's intended purpose for us? If we have fallen into spiritual death, can we be revived?

In 2016, Justin Smith from Pennsylvania was walking home in subzero temperatures. He was found the next day in the snow, unconscious, and with no pulse. When his father located him, he said, "He was blue in his face, he was lifeless. I checked for a pulse, I checked for a heartbeat, there was nothing."

How far gone is too far gone?

Justin's father called paramedics, they started chest compressions, and the ambulance headed towards Lehigh Valley Hospital in nearby Hazleton.

Emergency physician Dr. Gerald Coleman says of the incident, "You're not dead until you're warm and dead." Once Justin was warmed up through careful medical procedures, within 90 minutes, his heart began beating on its own.

Journalist Bobby Gavin was in his thirties, seemingly healthy, when a widowmaker heart attack took him down. As a registered nurse who didn't smoke, he had been told it "just wasn't possible" to have total blockages of the heart. Quick medical treatment allowed him to attend his honeymoon six months later.

Velma Thomas of West Virginia suffered a heart attack and was pronounced dead at the hospital. Seventeen hours later, she woke up and asked, "Where's my son?"

How far is too far gone for God to work a miracle in your life? "In him we have redemption through his blood" (Eph. 1:7). We cannot change on our own. And thankfully, it's not up to us. Our redemption comes through Christ, the cross, and the love of God. "For we are justified freely by his grace" (Rom. 3:24). Freely. There is no cost to us. We don't need to take out a loan, chastise our bodies, or subjugate ourselves to abject poverty. God wants to forgive our sins.

He "gave himself for us to redeem us" (Tit. 2:14).

Jesus loves us so much that he endured the cross to prove his love for us. It was a public shame-fest, observed and recorded for the world to view, and yet, Jesus considered it an honor to take our place.

Can you imagine the suffering he endured? "Christ also suffered … to bring you to God" (I Pet. 3:18). Jesus could, even before he was dragged into the Roman courts. In the garden, he was so stressed that his body leaked blood into his sweat, and it poured from his skin. He literally bled in prayer, asking the Father if there was any other way. And still, he said, "Not my will but yours be done" (Luke 22:42).

"The gift of God is eternal life in Christ (Rom. 6:23). Yes, life. Frozen in the snow? Yes, life. A widowmaker? Yes, life. Declared dead for seventeen hours? Yes, the gift of God is life. You may be blackened by sin, and your life may have taken you down dark roads that led to despair, but God says he is the lifegiver. "I am the resurrection and the life" (Jn. 11:25).

You are never too far gone to wear God's robe of purity and righteousness. He wants to wash you clean today.

The Cross Was Personal

I live by faith in the Son of God, who loved me and gave himself for me.

— Galatians 2:20 —

You were not yet born but were fully known by the Son of God at the creation of the world. He knew who you were before the first daybreak caressed the waters of the deep: your hopes, your fears, the times you would stumble, and the opportunities that would cross your path and allow you to achieve more than you ever thought you could.

When this verse says he "gave himself for me," that's not symbolic. The wording is literal. If you had been the only person in all of history to stumble, he would have still considered it worth the crushing pain of hanging on that cross to offer you a path to redemption.

Jesus died to provide atonement for our sins. He did so knowingly. He hung on the cross to pay the penalty for our wrongdoing, offering each person who walked the earth both past and present forgiveness and cleansing. We find evidence for his divine atonement in the Word of God in Ephesians 1:17: "In him we have redemption through his blood, the forgiveness of sins, in accordance with the riches of God's grace."

Jesus' death also offers reconciliation to God. Humanity's broken nature stirred hostility between God and mankind after the perfection of Eden and God's divine communion with his creation was shattered. The cross removed the wall of separation between God and his creation, bringing peace to those who placed their trust in him. "For God was pleased to have all his fullness dwell in him, and through him to reconcile to himself all things, whether on earth or in heaven, making peace by the blood of his cross" (Col. 1:19-20).

Through the redemption of the cross, we also receive freedom from sin's power. Believers no longer wear the heavy burden of shame and condemnation but are freed from the slavery of sin's crushing oppression. Romans 6:14 reveals: "For sin shall no longer be your master, because you are not under law, but under grace."

This isn't a temporary "fix-it" situation, a

counseling session, or a "clean-up-your-life" opportunity. When we receive Jesus as Lord of our life, we receive a new identity and being. Through Christ, we are literally reborn as a new creation, no longer dead in sin but alive in him. "Therefore, if anyone is in Christ, the new creation has come: The old has gone, the new is here!" (2 Cor. 5:17).

Through Jesus' suffering, we secure spiritual healing and wholeness. Where we were once spiritually broken, we are confident in the healing that can come from him alone. It is the reason that "He himself bore our sins in his body on the tree, so that we might die to sins and live for righteousness; [for] by his wounds you have been healed" (1 Pet. 2:24).

The Roman authorities thought the cross was their victory over the promise of salvation brought to the Jews by the man named Jesus. Instead, the entire world now had access to victory over death through the resurrection in which Jesus conquered death and assured us of eternal life. I Corinthians 15:5 exclaims, "Where, O death, is your victory? Where, O death, is your sting?"

At the moment of Jesus' death on the cross, we were adopted into God's Family. We were no longer inconsequential motes in his creation, bright in the moment but miniscule in his grand scheme. We were adopted into his family with all the rights and blessings of his children. We became children of the almighty God. "Yet to all who did receive him, to those who believed in his name, he gave the right to become children of God" (Jn. 1:12).

We are no longer bound by our flesh to the soil of this world. We receive divine justification and God's righteousness, not by our deeds, but through faith in Christ's work. In Ephesians 4:24, we read, "And [we will] be clothed with the new self, created to be like God in true righteousness and holiness."

Here's God connection to us today. Here's what he expects from us when he adopts us into his family. We are called to humble service. That's what the power of the cross creates in us when it flows in and through us. We "take up our cross," and in doing so, we prioritize God's glory and the needs of others. Our desires and needs become second place. This call is best stated in Luke 9:23: "If anyone would come after me, let him deny himself and take up his cross daily and follow me."

Finally, we are imbued with spiritual authority and

power, not of our own making, but that flows directly from the cross and Jesus' sacrifice. Giving ourselves to God's service is not a sign of weakness but of the power of God to transform our lives and defeat every attack the enemy might choose to bring against us. "For the word of the cross is folly to those who are perishing, but to us who are being saved it is the power of God" (1 Cor. 1:18).

— 2 —

The Weight We Carry

Why We Struggle with Forgiveness

Come to me, all you who are weary and burdened, and I will give you rest.

— Matthew 11:28 —

Forgiveness is a barrier that traps many of us. It is counterintuitive. Our brains are wired to put a wall between our pain and those who hurt us.

Fairy tales or film depictions of perfect resolutions don't help. Real conflict and deep hurt are harder to navigate than the pages of a book or in the ninety minutes of a feel-good action sequence. The negative emotions and the power of the offense hold sway over us. We still feel hurt or angry.

Here's the thing with forgiveness. It's not the same as reconciliation. It's about turning loose of the bitterness and the "hoping that they get what they deserve." Sometimes we think God sees us the same way, that we must "pay" for his forgiveness in some way. Instead, God says he will wipe the slate clean so that we can rest. Jesus has already paid the price, and all we need is to come to him.

Silent Shame, Loud Lies

When I kept silent, my bones wasted away through my groaning all day long.

— Psalm 32:3 —

Our social media-driven world places a huge premium on perfection. We are expected to model our lives after the glossy lifestyles of "influencers" who strive to only show the very best moments of their day. The struggle up the mountain? Unimportant if you are smiling when you stand on the summit. Hours of working your hair into an elaborate style? Only the final shot running your fingers through your tresses counts. Sending your kids out for the day so your house can look perfect for your photoshoot? Well, they can't stay inside. They'll mess everything up!

Shame also comes from the perfection we are expected to show the world. *Model Husband*, working long hours, still finding time for the kids, and able to take Mom on date nights every week. Who wouldn't want that life? Except that no one can stand up to that schedule. We fall off the pedestal and hope no cameras are nearby before we can climb back on.

Perhaps you are the *Stay at Home Mom*, breast feeding with a spotless kitchen. "Cleaning? I do that when the baby is down for her nap." Then we snap the picture for our post so that the world will know we have a perfect life.

When we can't keep up, we feel shame. Well-known professional organizer Marie Kondo made a success of minimalist living with her question: *Does it spark joy?* After having a child, she admitted her creed for organized living wasn't practical for the real world. How much deeper is our shame when we fail to live up to our boast of our "successful" Christian lifestyle? Many Christians struggle with things they did before (and sometimes after) coming to Christ. Yet we read: "Therefore, if anyone is in Christ, he is a new creation; the old has gone, the new has come!" (2 Cor. 5:17).

If shame lingers from past sexual relationships, promiscuity, or addictions, take heart in this verse: "But you were washed, you were sanctified, you were justified in the name of the Lord Jesus Christ and by the Spirit of our God" (1 Cor. 6:11). Our unresolved shame can lead to the persistent feeling that God is angry or that we are under constant judgment. Not so! If you feel condemned, repeat this verse daily: "So now there is no condemnation for those who belong to Christ Jesus" (Rom. 8:1).

If you can no longer live up to the perfectionism of social media, and its arbitrary standards have you feeling like a "bad" Christian, parent, or spouse because you don't meet some stranger's arbitrary standards, stand on this verse: "But he said to me, 'My grace is sufficient for you, for my power is made perfect in weakness'" (2 Cor. 12:9). If rejection and abandonment haunt your nights, and you carry the disgrace exhibited by the woman at the well, you can cast off your feelings of being unlovable or rejected. Read with me: "Those who look to him for help will be radiant with joy; no shadow of shame will darken their faces" (Ps. 34:5).

Even childhood trauma (everyone, it seems these days), disgrace from family members, or simply mistakes we made when we were younger and didn't understand their consequences don't have to be ours any longer. "Fear not; you will no longer live in shame. Don't be afraid; there is no more disgrace for you. You will no longer remember the shame of your youth …" (Is. 54:4).

But, we say, being forgiven by God doesn't wipe the record clean in other people's minds. They continually bring up the past. They don't realize how much their gossip hurts. When you fear public exposure or failure, and the reality of others knowing your secret sins or failures haunts you, take heart in this verse: "Instead of your shame, you will receive a double portion … and everlasting joy will be yours" (Is. 61:7). The lie of inadequacy and worthlessness from believing that you are not "good enough" or have no value is not God's plan for your life. "See what great love the Father has lavished on us, that we should be called children of God! And that is what we are!" (I Jn. 3:1).

Perhaps your shame doesn't come from you but from those around you or from your situation. You can't shake an ongoing hardship, whether it is emotional or material. Your health consistently lets you down, or a death in the family has your finances teetering on the brink. Maybe someone taunts you for your faith in Jesus. When you are suffering through each new trial, hold tight to this treasured verse: "However, if you suffer as a Christian, do not be ashamed, but praise God that you bear that name" (I Pet. 4:16).

Here is the last one, the big one, the silent shame that weighs most heavily on our shoulders: unconfessed sin. We can also read this as a guilty conscience. The shame might be real and even on-point, but instead of it leading to repentance, we feel forced to hide what we have done from even those closest to us. The Word gives a solution to our unconfessed sin so that we can walk with a clear conscience and our heads held high. "If we confess our sins, he is faithful and just and will forgive us our sins and purify us from all unrighteousness" (1 Jn. 1:9).

If we keep silent, our shame and guilt will eat at us. Our "bones will waste away," and we will lead a miserable life. If we confess our sins, we are made new in him and receive a fresh start on every count.

The Enemy's Accusation

> ... *The accuser of our brothers and sisters, who accuses them before our God day and night, has been hurled down.*
>
> — Revelation 12:10 —

The devil—also known as Lucifer or Satan—is a lion that attempts to devour the struggling Christian. If he can roar at us and keep us quivering under the guise of condemnation, we remain ineffective in our walk with Christ. Once we understand the ways the enemy attacks us, we can begin to see through his threats of intimidation.

God gives the evil one permission to enter heaven,

but for only one purpose. He can come before God to bring charges against the believers day and night. That's doesn't mean God accepts everything the devil says. Satan may have permission to stand in the presence of God, but the power of Jesus' sacrifice on the cross overpowers every word of the evil one. "For the accuser … has been hurled down" (Rev. 12:10).

When that doesn't work, Satan begins to question our sincerity in following Jesus. He suggests that our faith is only a result of God's blessings. "Strike everything he [Job] has, and he will surely curse you to your face" (Job 1:11). Privately he whispers to us that if we don't have prosperity, we must be unloved by God, suggesting that we are serving God only for his blessings rather than true love for him.

The devil will also use our past failures to remind us of our shame. He relentlessly brings up "dirty laundry" and old sins to make us feel condemned. Joshua, the High Priest, stood before God, repentant for the wrongdoing of Israel. "Then he showed me Joshua the high priest standing before the angel of the Lord, and Satan standing at his right side to accuse him. ² The Lord said to Satan, 'The Lord rebuke you, Satan! The Lord, who has chosen Jerusalem, rebuke you! Is not this man a burning stick snatched from the fire?'" (Zech. 3:1–2). When we are repentant before God, he clothes us in pure vestments, signifying forgiveness and restoration in our life. In the next two verses, we read of God's restorative power in Joshua's life. "Now Joshua was dressed in filthy clothes as he stood before the angel. ⁴ The angel said to those who were standing before him, 'Take off his filthy clothes.' Then he said to Joshua, 'See, I have taken away your sin, and I will put fine garments on you'" (Zech. 3:3-4) The devil loves to attack our standing before God and man. If he can get us to believe that we have no right to stand in God's presence due to our past sinfulness, we will never find the forgiveness to proclaim our Christian witness before man.

The devil wants us to doubt our forgiveness. He whispers that God's grace and past mercy do not apply to specific "unworthy" sinners (meaning YOU). "When he lies, he [Satan] speaks his native language, for he is a liar and the father of lies" (Jn. 8:44). He sends internal thoughts of despair to destroy our spiritual peace and create isolation from our fellow believers. However, there is one in whom we can place our faith. "Who then is the one who condemns? No one. Christ Jesus who died—more than that, who was raised to life—is at the right hand of God and is also interceding for us" (Rom. 8:34). If you feel self-condemnation, and if the devil tries to scrutinize every motive and feeling to convince you that you are disqualified from God's work, know this: "If our hearts condemn us, we know that God is greater than our hearts, and he knows everything" (I Jn. 3:20).

The devil also loves to plant suspicion among believers by whispering in our ear. He accuses other Christians by subtly planting suspicions about their motives. They can be doing what God wants and requires of them, but the devil—who is the father of lies—suggests they are doing it for their own good or to gain from it financially. He hopes to create division among the believers, and we must not listen to him. "By examining him yourself you will be able to learn the truth about all these charges we are bringing against him" (Acts 24:8).

If that doesn't work, he will use others to accuse us. He will influence people with lies and whispers to slander or discredit our reputation. Once the trust is broken between us and the people around us, he hopes our testimony will be shattered into dust. We must stand before him and, in the name of the Lord, rebuke the lies of the devil. "You, however, know all about my teaching, my way of life, my purpose, faith, patience, love, endurance, [11] persecutions, [and] sufferings …" (2 Tim. 3:10-11).

Finally, if the devil can't get through to us, he will endeavor to distort God's character. He will accuse God before us, suggesting he is an angry judge with only one agenda: waiting for us to fail. Wear the wrong shirt, step into the wrong restaurant, click on the wrong TV show … if we show up in heaven with the least sin unforgiven, we will be cast into hell. After all, God doesn't want the best for us. He only wishes to satisfy his own twisted desires. We saw the devil do this to Eve in the Garden of Eden. "'You will not certainly die,' the serpent said to the woman. [5] 'For God knows that when you eat from it your eyes will be opened, and you will be like God, knowing good and evil'" (Gen 3:4-5).

When We Can't Forgive Ourselves

If our hearts condemn us, we know that God

is greater than our hearts ...

— 1 John 3:20 —

Self-reliance can become a hindrance to forgiving ourselves when we stumble. We struggle to accept God's forgiveness and attempt to earn back his grace. We fail to comprehend that forgiveness is God's unmerited gift, one we cannot earn but only accept. "Do not think of yourself more highly than you ought, but ... in accordance with the faith God has distributed to each of you" (Rom. 12:3). When we think we can overcome our failings without the help of God, we become too dependent on "works" (counseling, restitution, or self-help sessions) and don't give God credit for loving us as his children.

We demonstrate unbelief in Christ's sufficiency. We refuse to move past guilt unless we can provide our own solution. This can be a form of unbelief, effectively saying that Jesus' sacrifice on the cross was not enough to cover our sin. We must return to Jesus' final words: "It is finished" (Jn. 19:30), where we learn that there is no further payment required for our sins.

If we listen to the accuser, spiritual opposition by the devil will nurture our constant feelings of self-condemnation. God convicts us so that he can lead us to repentance. Satan accuses us of transgressions (real and imagined) to lead us to despair. We see this in Revelation 12:10 which describes Satan as "the accuser of our brothers and sisters, who accuses them before our God day and night."

Self-righteous standards can also impede us from forgiving ourselves. Is it possible to hold themselves to higher standards than God does? Yes, if we refuse to accept God's forgiveness because we have failed to maintain our own "perfect" ideals. No one can be perfectly sin-free, for we are all human. "For all have sinned and fall short of the glory of God" (Rom. 3:23). No one can adhere to a standard of perfection on their own.

In today's world of social media and the false standards of perfection foisted upon us, we can fall into seeking others' approval. Rather than letting God's forgiveness be our way forward, we place our worldly reputation or another person's approval before God's forgiveness. We wail, "What will people think if they find out? So-and-so won't invite me to any more parties ..." or some such. We forget God's command that: "You shall have no other gods before me" (Ex. 20:3). We push aside his reminder that his opinion comes before all others. He is the ultimate authority.

When we berate ourselves for stumbling (a form of grief for our perceived failure), we make the mistake of confusing our private grief for the godly grief that brings true repentance. Godly grief (or regret and shame) leads us to change our behavior and lifestyle. Worldly grief only leads to spiritual death and hopelessness. "Godly sorrow brings repentance that leads to salvation and leaves no regret, but worldly sorrow brings death" (2 Cor. 7:10).

We mustn't let our mistakes define us. We are children of God. When our misplaced identity brings on low self-worth, we feel that we do not deserve God's forgiveness and freedom from shame. "See what great love the Father has lavished on us, that we should be called children of God! And that is what we are!" (1 Jn. 3:1). We are encouraged to see ourselves as God sees us. The world sees who we used to be, not who we are in God. The end of this verse doubles down with: "The reason the world does not know us is that it did not know him."

We must focus on truth over feelings. We must strive to set aside our present emotions and stand on the promises found in Scripture. Guilt often persists because individuals prioritize their emotions rather than step out on the promises found in the Word. Remember this verse? "If our hearts condemn us, we know that God is greater than our hearts, and he knows everything" (I Jn. 3:20). When God offers his forgiveness and we accept, he doesn't even remember that our wrongdoing happened.

Even though God's forgiveness is complete, guilt can haunt us if we have not yet attempted to make amends with the people we harmed. "Therefore, if you are offering your gift at the altar and remember that your brother or sister has something against you, [24] leave your gift in front of the altar. First go and be reconciled to them; then come and offer your gift" (Matt. 5:23–24). It's amazing how much just "clearing the air" can change the level of guilt we carry.

Have you assumed the role of judge in your life? If you've refused to accept God's pardon for your past failures, you have ascended to the throne, effectively claiming that your verdict of guilty is greater than

God's verdict of justified through the saving grace of Jesus. "There is therefore now no condemnation for those who are in Christ Jesus" (Rom. 8:1). By accepting God's pardon, you allow God's justification to clear your self-defeating thoughts and prepare you to enter a better life in him.

The Trap of Legalism

It is for freedom that Christ has set us free. Stand firm, then, and do not let yourselves be burdened again by a yoke of slavery.

— Galatians 5:1 —

We fall into modern legalism when we overly focus on outward rules and human traditions rather than the inward change that comes through faith in Jesus. When we slavishly follow the law, we operate under the belief that we can earn or maintain merit before God.

Here are ten legalism traps modern Christians must avoid:

We cannot earn salvation through good works.

The belief that we can keep religious laws or perform good deeds to secure our standing before God leads us astray. "For it is by grace you have been saved, through faith ... not by works, so that no one can boast" (Eph. 2:8-9).

When we treat man-made rules such as specific dress codes, musical styles, or diet as biblical absolutes, we are elevating human preference to divine law. "They worship me in vain; their teachings are merely human rules" (Matt. 15:9).

We must not put visible conformity above our internal spiritual health. Not drinking, smoking, or missing church can be markers for our spiritual health, but to focus only on these outward appearances over our relationship with Christ is a mistake. "For the Lord sees not as man sees: man looks on the outward appearance, but the Lord looks on the heart" (1 Sam. 16:7).

We must avoid self-righteous comparison at all costs. When we follow a rule that others break, and we become judgmental toward them, we have broken one of God's primary rules. Feeling superior to others can lead to a judgmental spirit. Remember the Pharisee's prayer: "God, I thank you that I am not like other people ..." (Luke 18:11).

Our Christian walk cannot be performance-based. We are not "more saved" when succeeding in our Chistian walk and "less saved" (or condemned) after a failure. The same free grace that covered you at salvation is still available for you when you stumble. "Therefore, there is now no condemnation for those who are in Christ Jesus" (Rom. 8:1).

We must be careful not to add conditions to the free grace offered by God at the cross. Mixing our faith with additional requirements for justification, such as extra hours of prayer or working the serving line at the downtown mission, strangles the joy of the gospel. "Knowing that a person is not justified by the works of the law but through faith in Jesus Christ" (Gal. 2:16).

On the opposite side, looking for a loophole is another dangerous legalism. If we follow the letter of the law while violating its actual intent or neglect weightier matters like love, we have failed in our Christian walk. "You give a tenth ... But you have neglected the more important matters of the law—justice, mercy and faithfulness" (Matt. 23:23).

When we impose our personal convictions (e.g.,

no movies or specific schooling choices) on others as if they are God's spoken word, we become guilty of binding other people's consciences with our convictions. "Who are you to judge someone else's servant? To his own master he stands or falls" (Rom. 14:4).

In American culture, pulling ourselves up by our bootstraps is admired, and relying on self-effort rather than the Holy Spirit can feel natural. However, if we attempt to live out our Christian walk by willpower, we begin to honor the flesh instead of wrapping ourselves in divine grace. "Are you so foolish? After beginning by means of the Spirit, are you now trying to finish by means of the flesh?" (Gal. 3:3).

Finally, it is heartbreaking when Christians sacrifice relationships for rule-keeping. We demand strict adherence to traditions, even placing our traditions over the needs of neighbors or community. "Oh, them? I wouldn't sit in the same service with someone like that! Don't they have any proper clothing?" Or even, "It's Sunday. Don't they know they shouldn't be at the mall on God's day?" The Word tells us: "The Sabbath was made for man, not man for the Sabbath" (Mk. 2:27).

Carrying What Jesus Took

Surely he took up our pain and bore our suffering ...

— Isaiah 53:4 —

In Christian theology, a cross can be defined as a voluntary choice to obey God's will at a personal cost, such as enduring ridicule for your faith or giving up your personal time to serve at the local mission for the homeless. True discipleship symbolizes a willingness to die to our own desires and reputation to follow Jesus. However, an unnecessary cross refers to heavy burdens or suffering that Jesus never intended for believers to carry.

Carrying guilt and shame for sins that have already been confessed and forgiven is a cross that doesn't belong on our shoulders. The Word says: "As far as the east is from the west, so far has he removed our transgressions from us" (Ps. 103:12).

Worry and anxiety are nothing more than shouldering the weight of future uncertainties instead of trusting God. Jesus bore your worries while he hung on the cross. It's time to turn them over to him. "Cast all your anxiety on him because he cares for you" (I Pet. 5:7).

We are not responsible for the sins of others. When we fill our backpacks with the weight of the poor choices and sins of those around us, whether they be spouses, children, coworkers or friends, our own testimony can lose its joy. "For each one should carry their own load" (Gal. 6:5).

Jesus tossed out the restrictive practices of the clergy. We no longer need to shoulder the heavy weight of man-made religious rules and moralistic policing. "They tie up heavy, cumbersome loads and put them on other people's shoulders, but they themselves are not willing to lift a finger to move them" (Matt. 23:4).

Bitterness against those who've wronged us is corrosive to our relationship with Christ. When we hold onto resentment, our unforgiveness acts as a heavy, demoralizing internal weight. "Get rid of all bitterness, rage and anger, brawling and slander, along with every form of malice" (Eph. 4:31).

We must not become responsible for other people's financial decisions. When we place the legal and emotional weight of another person's debt into our backpack, we take on financial suretyship. We guarantee that another person will meet their financial obligations, such as when co-signing on a loan. The Word says otherwise. "Whoever becomes surety for a stranger will surely suffer, but whoever refuses to shake hands in pledge is safe" (Prov. 11:15).

We cannot assume the burden of spiritual pride. If we attempt to maintain a perfect appearance, essentially one-upping each other spiritually, we will fall victim to spiritual exhaustion. "For if anyone thinks he is something, when he is nothing, he deceives himself" (Gal. 6:3).

Everyone's pain is not ours to wipe away. We can only point them to Christ. We must be the signpost, and it is up to them to make the turn toward Jesus. "Come to me, all you who are weary and burdened, and I will give you rest" (Matt. 11:28).

America faces a mega-church crisis based on prosperity. The stress and distraction caused by excessive focus on possessions can stifle our growth in Christ. "Then he said to them, 'Watch out! Be on your guard against all kinds of greed; life does not consist in an abundance of possessions'" (Luke 12:15).

God's forgiveness is absolute. When we give in to prolonged guilt and refuse to accept God's mercy after repentance, we become mired in emotional agony that Jesus never intended. "If we confess our sins, he is faithful and just and will forgive us our sins and purify us from all unrighteousness" (I Jn. 1:9).

Jesus came to "take it all." He desires to shoulder those things that are about to tip us over the edge. When we walk with him, he wants to carry his portion of our problems, and that means all of them.

— 3 —

Washed Clean

The Power of the Blood of Jesus

In him we have redemption through his blood, the forgiveness of sins, in accordance with the riches of God's grace ...

— Ephesians 1:7 —

Memory stains us. There's a reason Lot's wife turned to a pillar of salt when leaving her home in Sodom. Mentally, she couldn't let go, no matter how bad her past experiences were. It literally froze her into inaction, and she was left behind when Lot and his daughters fled to the nearby town of Zoar.

Here's how I had memories (especially bad ones) described to me. Each day is a film set. At the end of the day, filming is wrapped, the set is broken down, and the celluloid is canned and put on a shelf. We can't go back and retake any of the scenes, only watch replays of what was filmed.

And here's the important part: we don't have to rewatch any of it. We can hit the stop button. Place the video on the shelf. Close the cabinet. Move forward. Focus on today's soundstage and see where it takes us. Never become a pillar of salt staring back at what used to be.

When we refuse to rewatch the movies of our life, we also leave the emotions and traumas of those days on the shelf. That's what Ephesians 1:7 says to us. Redemption, forgiveness … washed clean. If we don't rewatch our past mistakes, well, God isn't rewatching them, either. He sees our future and what we can make of today, tomorrow, and the day after that.

The Price Was Paid

Without the shedding of blood there is no forgiveness.

— Hebrews 9:22 —

In the Bible, the shedding of blood is a fundamental requirement for the forgiveness and covering (or atonement) of sins. This principle is established in Leviticus 17:11, which states: "For the life of the flesh is in the blood … it is the blood that makes atonement for the soul." Let's look at how this practice progressed throughout the Word from God's earliest interaction with humanity to the awe-inspiring sacrifice of Jesus as he hung on the cross to give his life as the ultimate sacrifice for humanity.

Animal Skins for Adam and Eve

Our first instance of blood being shed to cover sin occurred after the Fall. We know the story of Eve and the fruit from the Tree of the Knowledge of Good and Evil, and that Adam joined Eve in her sin. God rejected the couple's attempt to cover themselves with fig leaves and instead provided garments made from animal skins. Adam and Eve tried to atone for their sin by human means, which is futile. "The Lord God made garments of skin for Adam and his wife and clothed them" (Gen. 3:21). Only God can cover and wash us clean from our wrongdoing.

Abel's Sacrifice

As one of Adam and Eve's firstborn children, Abel aligned himself with God's intent and offered a blood sacrifice from the firstborn of his flock. We read that God looked kindly on Abel's offering and accepted his sacrifice. This blood offering demonstrated his humility and faith in trusting God to redeem him from sin.

God had shed the first blood offering, and now, mankind shed the second. "Abel also brought of the firstborn of his flock and of their fat. And the Lord respected Abel and his offering" (Gen. 4:4).

The Passover Lamb

In Egypt, the Israelites were being squeezed by the fist of Pharoah. Moses was in negotiations between

God and Pharoah, and the final phase of the negotiations was the death of the firstborn of every family in the land. Even the Israelites ... except. The Israelites were commanded to slaughter a spotless lamb and apply its blood to their doorposts to protect them from the judgment of death. The sacrifice served as a substitute for their firstborn, becoming a likeness of the blood of Christ shed upon the cross. "The blood shall be a sign for you on the houses where you are. And when I see the blood, I will pass over you" (Ex. 12:13). When we have the blood of Christ covering us, we are protected from the ravages of sin.

The Day of Atonement (Yom Kippur)

God widened his umbrella. He needed an ongoing atonement that covered all his children. Once a year, the high priest would offer the blood of a bull and a goat in the Temple. This practice not only atoned for his own sins but included the sins of the entire nation. The blood was shed before God in the Holy of Holies. "For on this day atonement will be made for you to cleanse you, and you will be clean from all your sins before the Lord" (Lev. 16:30).

The Sacrifice of Jesus Christ

In the New Testament, Jesus shed His blood as the final and perfect sacrifice. Unlike animal blood, which could only cover sins temporarily, Christ's blood provides eternal redemption and remission for all who believe. The set is broken, the film is canned, and it is sealed with the redeeming blood of Christ and set on a shelf for the rest of time. We move forward onto a new soundstage, wearing a spotless robe and ready for whatever God has for us on this day. "For this is my blood of the new testament, which is shed for many for the remission of sins" (Matt. 26:28).

Atonement Once for All

We have been made holy through the sacrifice of Jesus once for all.

— Hebrews 10:10 —

Biblical atonement represents reconciliation

between God and humanity. While the work of atonement was completed by Jesus Christ once and for all, individuals can enhance its benefits through specific spiritual pathways.

When we place our faith in Jesus Christ, our initial atonement is received by believing in the sacrifice and resurrection of Jesus as the only means of salvation. "Whom God put forward as a propitiation by his blood, to be received by faith" (Rom. 3:25). Sincere repentance and atonement involve a change of mind and heart. We must actively turn away from our sin and back toward God. "Repent, then, and turn to God, so that your sins may be wiped out" (Acts 3:19).

The Apostle Peter was one of Jesus' closest disciples. Yet, despite his protests of loyalty, Peter denied knowing Jesus three times during the night of his arrest. After the resurrection, Jesus met Peter by the Sea of Galilee and restored him to fellowship. "He said to him the third time, 'Simon, son of John, do you love me?' … and he [Peter] said to him, 'Lord, you know everything; you know that I love you.' Jesus said to him, 'Feed my sheep'" (Jn. 21:17).

We must be honest before God. He requires a straightforward confession of our sins rather than an attempt to conceal them or excuse them as being "only human." God then welcomes us to his companionship. "If we confess our sins, he is faithful and just to forgive us our sins and to cleanse us from all unrighteousness" (1 Jn. 1:9).

Then, through propitiation (or appeasement of God's wrath) at the mercy seat of God, he covers our sins with the sacrifice of Christ. "He is the propitiation for our sins ... [and] for the sins of the whole world" (1 Jn. 2:2). We receive an exchange of our guilt for the righteousness of Christ. "For our sake he made him to be sin who knew no sin, so that in him we might become the righteousness of God" (2 Cor. 5:21).

God ransoms us through the power of redemption with the payment of Jesus' blood shed on the cross. The sacrifice Jesus willingly offered buys believers back from slavery to sin and spiritual death. "In him we have redemption through his blood, the forgiveness of sins, in accordance with the riches of God's grace" (Eph. 1:7). Through God's ransoming power, he removes the enmity between God and man, and we are reconciled with him in a relationship of peace. "Having made peace through the blood of his cross, by him to reconcile all things unto himself" (Col. 1:20).

God cancels the legal record of debt that stands against humanity (and therefore us) because of man's transgressions: "He forgave us all our sins, having canceled the charge of our legal indebtedness … nailing it to the cross" (Col. 2:13–14) and cleanses us with a spiritual washing that purifies our conscience from the stain of sin. "Wash me thoroughly from my iniquity, and cleanse me from my sin" (Ps. 51:2). It's not too much to say that our ultimate atonement is received through the healing that flows from the physical and spiritual suffering Christ endured on behalf of his followers and all those who would come to believe in him throughout the centuries. "He was pierced for our transgressions … and with his wounds we are healed" (Is. 53:5).

How can we know our atonement is a real, factual part of our Christian experience, different from the sacrificial practices of the Old Testament?

First, we display true repentance as exhibited through regret for our sins, while offering a confession of those sins to God, and praying a prayer for his forgiveness. We also make a firm resolve not to repeat our sins. This is evidenced by a change in our behavior as we strive to emulate the example of holy living given to us by Jesus in the Bible.

Second, we substantiate the sacrificial blood sacrifice of the Old Testament with charity and kind deeds toward the less fortunate and needy. In essence, we are sacrificing our own time and resources as a proof of concept that we have accepted God's atonement.

Third, we participate in the Eucharist, or Communion, and are publicly baptized to symbolize our renewed covenant with God. In other words, we make a public confession of our new faith in God.

Finally, we fast and spend time in prayer. Essentially, we deprive ourselves of physical pleasures such as certain foods or "me time" to focus on spiritual preparation as a form of atonement.

Christ's sacrifice on the cross is our ultimate atonement, but when we take part in moving closer to him through acts of sacrificial atonement in our daily walk with him, we are reminded of what Jesus did for us, and we strengthen our bond with him.

No More Condemnation

There is now no condemnation for those who are in Christ Jesus.

— Romans 8:1 —

The Bible contains numerous accounts of individuals who received profound forgiveness after significant failures. We can read into these stories the biblical themes of redemption and grace. I want to share with you seven examples of forgiven people in the Bible that will bring home the level of compassion that Jesus continues to offer to us today.

King David is the only example I will pull from the Old Testament. Despite being a "man after God's own heart," David committed adultery with Bathsheba and arranged the murder of her husband, Uriah. Even in David's time, this was a heinous disregard of humanity by the leader of God's chosen people. Yet, when confronted by the prophet Nathan, David repented sincerely. "Then David said to Nathan, 'I have sinned against the Lord.' Nathan replied, 'The Lord has taken away your sin. You are not going to die'" (2 Sam. 12:13).

The Apostle Paul was originally a fierce persecutor

of the early church known as Saul of Tarsus. As Saul, he was present at the stoning of Stephen and sought to imprison Christians. He experienced a dramatic conversion on the road to Damascus and took on the name Paul to demonstrate his conversion and new belief in Christ. "Even though I was once a blasphemer and a persecutor and a violent man, I was shown mercy because I acted in ignorance and unbelief" (1 Tim. 1:13).

The woman caught in adultery was brought before Jesus by religious leaders who wanted to stone her according to the law. She faced certain death. However, Jesus challenged her accusers and ultimately extended mercy to her. "'Then neither do I condemn you,' Jesus declared. 'Go now and leave your life of sin'" (Jn. 8:11).

The Parable of the Prodigal Son is one of Jesus' most famous parables. A son squanders his inheritance on wild living and returns home in shame, hoping only to be a servant. Instead, his father welcomes him back with a celebration. "But the father said to his servants, 'Quick! Bring the best robe and put it on him … For this son of mine was dead and is alive again; he was lost and is found'" (Luke 15:22-24).

The thief on the cross was being crucified next to Jesus. He acknowledged his own guilt and asked Jesus to remember him. Jesus granted him immediate forgiveness and assurance of salvation. "Jesus answered him, 'Truly I tell you, today you will be with me in paradise'" (Luke 23:43).

I want to wind up with Zacchaeus, a wealthy tax collector often despised by his community for dishonesty. To me, the story of Zacchaeus resonates more for what Jesus says than who Zacchaeus was. Zacchaeus sought to see Jesus in Jericho. After Jesus visited his home, Zacchaeus repented of his greed and promised to make restitution. Here we hear the words of the Master: "Jesus said to him, 'Today salvation has come to this house ... For the Son of Man came to seek and to save the lost'" (Luke 19:9-10).

In none of these examples do we see God wagging his finger, saying, "I told you so," or suggesting that he intends some sort of retribution for the wrongdoing. He simply forgives and moves on. That's the power of the blood Jesus shed on the cross. When we are washed in the blood (absolved of our sins), we emerge clean and spotless before God and never need to look back.

A New Creation Arises

If anyone is in Christ, the new creation has come ...

— 2 Corinthians 5:17 —

Being a "new creation" in Christ signifies a radical, spiritual transformation that redefines a person's identity, values, and purpose. This change is not merely behavioral but an internal renewal initiated by the Holy Spirit.

While we are sanctified immediately, no one receives instant perfection, as this is a gradual, lifelong process. We continue to struggle until our character is truly transformed into the likeness of God.

Here are 17 ways a modern Christian can live out this new identity:

Recognize that you are a beloved, chosen child of God, no longer defined by your past sins or worldly standards. Acknowledge your new identity before the world. "If anyone is in Christ, the ... old has gone, the new is here" (2 Cor. 5:17).

Consciously shift from worldly ways of thinking to God's perspective through consistent meditation on scripture. You renew your mind through time in the Word and in prayer. "Be transformed by the renewing of your mind. Then you will be able to test and approve what God's will is" (Rom. 12:2).

Ensure that God is the central focus of your life, letting your values and schedules fall into place around him. When you prioritize God in your life, everything pales next to him. "Seek first his kingdom and his righteousness, and all these things will be given to you as well" (Matt. 6:33).

Shift your primary motivation from personal desire to glorifying the One who died for you. When you live for Christ and not for self, every part of who you are changes. "Those who live should no longer live for themselves but for him who died for them and was raised again" (2 Cor. 5:15).

Actively identify and abandon old habits, sinful patterns, and corrupt mindsets from your former life. You are putting off your old self and taking on the mantle of Christ. "To put off your old self, ... and to put on the new self, created to be like God in true righteousness and holiness" (Eph. 4:22-24).

Commit to the lifelong process of sanctification. Seek spiritual growth by delving daily into the knowledge of Christ so that you can become like him. "Grow in the grace and knowledge of our Lord and Savior Jesus Christ" (2 Pet. 3:18).

Allow the Holy Spirit to produce new traits like love, joy, and self-control to replace earthly desires. "The fruit of the Spirit is love, joy, peace, forbearance, kindness, goodness, faithfulness, gentleness and self-control. Against such things there is no law" (Gal. 5:22-23).

Release grudges and past hurts, forgiving others as God has forgiven you. When you extend radical forgiveness, you begin to shine with the purity of Christ. "Bear with each other and forgive one another if any of you has a grievance against someone. Forgive as the Lord forgave you" (Col. 3:13).

View others through spiritual eyes rather than a worldly point of view. When you walk in compassion, you show love even to your enemies. "From now on we regard no one from a worldly point of view" (2 Cor. 5:16),

Embrace a life of prayer. Develop a constant, personal dialogue with God to receive guidance and strength for daily living. "Rejoice always, [17] pray continually, [18] give thanks in all circumstances; for this is God's will for you in Christ Jesus" (1 Thess. 5:16-18).

Immerse yourself in the Bible daily to let its truths reshape your character and choices. "Jesus said, 'If you hold to my teaching, you are really my disciples. [32] Then you will know the truth, and the truth will set you free'" (Jn. 8:31-32).

Connect with a local church for support, accountability, and mutual encouragement in faith. "Not giving up meeting together … but encouraging one another" (Heb. 10: 25).

Use your life and new nature to actively love and meet the needs of those around you. Serving others selflessly is a sign of your new creation in Christ. "You, my brothers and sisters, were called to … serve one another humbly in love" (Gal. 5:13).

Exercise your spiritual gifts as you discover and use the unique abilities God has given you. You are empowered to build and edify his church. "Each of you should use whatever gift you have received to serve others, as faithful stewards of God's grace" (1 Pet. 4:10).

Live as a representative of God's kingdom, sharing the message of reconciliation with the world. As an ambassador for Christ, you become the hand of God to those you help. "We are therefore Christ's ambassadors, as though God were making his appeal through us" (2 Cor. 5:20).

Rely on the indwelling Holy Spirit to overcome sinful impulses that previously controlled you. The Spirit's power will enable you to become the master of your desires. Your impulses will no longer dominate you, and you will be able to resist temptation. "For sin shall no longer be your master, because you are not under the law, but under grace" (Rom. 6:14).

Maintain an eternal perspective. When we focus on the unseen and eternal spiritual realities rather than being consumed by our temporary, earthly troubles, we learn that in Jesus, we have all we need. "For our light and momentary troubles are achieving for us an eternal glory ... so we fix our eyes not on what is seen, but on what is unseen" (2 Cor. 4:17-18).

Clothed in Righteousness

For he has clothed me with garments of

salvation and arrayed me in a robe of his righteousness ...

— Isaiah 61:10 —

In the Bible, being clothed in righteousness serves as a metaphor for a divine transformation where God replaces human sinfulness with his own holiness.

In Isaiah 61:10, not only is the prophet clothed in righteousness, he delights in what the Lord has done for him. "I delight greatly in the Lord; my soul rejoices in my God. For he has clothed me with garments of salvation and arrayed me in a robe of his righteousness."

Job 29:14 gives us Job's defense against his accusers: "I put on righteousness as my clothing; justice was my robe and my turban." He knows God has him covered with his hand.

Psalm 132:9 is an appeal of praise to God, a song to glorify the Lord. "May your priests be clothed with your righteousness; may your faithful people sing for joy."

Ephesians 6:14 describes the full armor of God and its importance for all Christians. "Stand firm then, with the belt of truth buckled around your waist, with the breastplate of righteousness in place."

The passage in which we find this next verse talks about our position as children of God. Galatians 3:27 specifically says, "For all of you who were baptized into Christ have clothed yourselves with Christ." Jesus is revealed as our righteousness.

Romans 13:14 also refers to Christ as our righteousness. "Rather, clothe yourselves with the Lord Jesus Christ, and do not think about how to gratify the desires of the flesh."

When we cast off our old self, Ephesians 4:24 says that our new self is clothed in God's righteousness. We are to "to put on the new self, created to be like God in true righteousness and holiness."

Revelation 19:8 describes our righteousness as fine linen. "Fine linen, bright and clean, was given her to wear."

Zechariah 3:4 reveals the purification and absolution of Joshua as he stands in a vision before the Lord. "The angel said to those who were standing before him, 'Take off his filthy clothes.' Then he said to Joshua, 'See, I have taken away your sin, and I will put fine garments on you.'"

Philippians 3:9 tells us our righteousness does not come from our own efforts or through religion. "Not having a righteousness of my own that comes from the law, but that which is through faith in Christ."

We see the great multitude in their white robes of righteousness in Revelation 7:9. "There before me was a great multitude that no one could count, from every nation, tribe, people and language, standing before the throne and before the Lamb. They were wearing white robes and were holding palm branches in their hands."

2 Corinthians 5:21 points to Christ as our only source of righteousness. "God made him who had no sin to be sin for us, so that in him we might become the righteousness of God."

Colossians 3:12 spells out the attributes of righteousness that God expects of his children. "Therefore, as God's chosen people, holy and dearly loved, clothe yourselves with compassion, kindness, humility, gentleness and patience."

Revelation 19:14 reveals the coming of the Lord in holy righteousness. "The armies of heaven were following him, riding on white horses and dressed in fine linen, white and clean."

Let's turn back to the earliest example of God clothing humanity in righteousness in Genesis 3:21: "The Lord God made garments of skin for Adam and his wife and clothed them." We receive the righteousness of God because we are loved by him.

Job stated he "put on righteousness, and it clothed me" to attest *to his upright life and the just way he treated those* around him.

In a vision, Joshua the High Priest had his sinful garments *replaced with clean, rich robes.*

The great multitude in Revelation were seen *wearing white robes, representing their righteousness* gained through Christ.

Additional biblical examples of people God clothed in righteousness reveal even more:

Abraham's faith was "credited to him as righteousness," *signifying his spiritual standing before God.*

The prodigal son was given the "best robe" upon his return, *symbolizing his restoration and renewed standing.*

Noah, Daniel, and Job are mentioned in Ezekiel as individuals whose *own righteousness would save them.*

Now ask yourself the hard question. **Where do**

you stand in God's righteousness? Jesus has paid the price already, and you are included. He no longer condemns you. Once you decide to trust him and accept his offer of salvation, a new creature arises from the ashes of your old life.

If you want to be clothed in the righteous of God, you can receive it today.

— 4 —

The Gift You Must Receive

Accepting God's Forgiveness

If we confess our sins, he is faithful and just to forgive …

— 1 John 1:9 —

Salvation seems too easy.

"What? All we do is say yes? And it's free? Okay, then, what's the catch? I know there must be one somewhere. This will cost on the back end. What's the real price I'll be asked to pay?"

Agreed, there is a cost to salvation. It's not what you think, though. We can be a mess, with our lives in a scramble, and still, Jesus loves us. He will never say, "After you've cured that addiction ..." or "About that divorce ..." or "I've been thinking about your yearly bonus ... the church auditorium does need a new roof ..."

In this chapter, I want to spend time looking at the gift of salvation and what it ensues. Yes, it is a gift, but as with any gift, there are some conditions. You can refuse a gift. You can mislead the gift giver. You can set it on a shelf and never put it to use. You can even thank the wrong person. Worst of all, you can commit the ultimate infraction by considering the gift inadequate and expecting more.

There's a host of ways we can mess up receiving a gift, and the gift of salvation is the one we cannot afford to bumble.

It's vital to get it right the first time.

Come As You Are

Come, all you who are thirsty, come to the waters; and you who have no money, come, buy and eat! Come, buy wine and milk without money and without cost.

— Isaiah 55:1 —

We can feel uncomfortable in the church: criticized, looked down upon. And perhaps we've done things that warrant that. Jesus frequently engaged with and accepted individuals marginalized or condemned by religious authorities. His mission focused on reaching those in need of spiritual healing.

Jesus invited Matthew, a tax collector and a man considered a traitorous sinner by many Jews, to follow him and later dined at his house with other worldly people. He didn't ask Matthew to change his lifestyle before breaking bread with him. To the Pharisees, he said, "For I have not come to call the righteous, but sinners" (Matt. 9: 13).

When religious leaders brought a woman caught in sin for execution, Jesus defended her from her accusers and offered her mercy instead of condemnnation. He didn't wag his finger at her but accepted her as she was. "'Then neither do I condemn you,' Jesus declared. 'Go now and leave your life of sin'"

(Jn. 8:11).

Jesus stayed at the home of another tax collector, Zacchaeus, this time a chief in his field. The crowds publicly grumbled that he was the guest of a sinner. Surely Jesus must know who this man was. Yet, Jesus replied, "Today salvation has come to this house … [10] For the Son of Man came to seek and to save the lost" (Luke 19:9-10).

Jesus initiated a conversation with a Samaritan woman at a well who had been married multiple times and was currently living with a man not her husband, breaking the social and religious barriers of her day. Through their interaction, many of the local townspeople came to believe in him. "And because of his words many more became believers" (Jn. 4:41).

The woman who anointed Jesus was known for her sinful life, yet she washed Jesus' feet with tears and anointed them with oil. Jesus praised her faith and forgave her. "Your faith has saved you; go in peace" (Luke 7:50).

In his final hours as he hung on the cross, Jesus accepted the thief on the cross next to him when he asked for mercy. Jesus promised him a place in paradise. "Truly I tell you, today you will be with me in paradise" (Luke 23:43).

Jesus was frequently criticized by the Pharisees for having table fellowship with individuals labeled as social and moral outcasts, i.e. publicans and sinners. "The Pharisees and the teachers of the law muttered, 'This man welcomes sinners and eats with them'" (Luke 15:2). Yet in the healing of the paralytic, before physically healing the man, Jesus first addressed his spiritual need by declaring his sins forgiven, asserting his authority to accept and restore sinners. "When Jesus saw their faith, he said to the paralyzed man, 'Son, your sins are forgiven'" (Mk. 2:5).

Jesus also included those in secular authority over the nation of the Jews. He marveled at the faith of a gentile soldier, a Centurion of the occupying Roman forces, and granted his request for healing for his servant. "Then Jesus said to the centurion, 'Go! Let it be done just as you believed it would'" (Matt. 8:13).

Even when we fail Jesus, he invites us back into his presence as seen in the restoration of Peter. After Peter denied Jesus three times—a deep moral failure—Jesus specifically sought him out to restore and recommission him to spread the gospel and share the good news of Jesus' message of redemption.

"Then he said to him, 'Follow me!'" (John 21:19).

Confession, Not Perfection

Whoever conceals their sins does not prosper, but the one who confesses and renounces them finds mercy.

— Proverbs 28:13 —

Confession plays a significant role in receiving forgiveness and restoration. Throughout the Bible, individuals or groups who confessed their sins and were forgiven exemplify the future redemption provided by the cross and the sacrificial death of our Lord.

After his sin with Bathsheba, King David confessed to the prophet Nathan, saying, "I have sinned against the Lord." When he is absolved by Nathan, David cries: "Deliver me from the guilt of bloodshed, O God, you who are God my Savior, and my tongue will sing of your righteousness" (Ps. 51:14).

In Jesus' parable of the prodigal son, the son

confesses his sin and unworthiness to his father, who welcomes him back with open arms. "But the father said to his servants, 'Quick! Bring the best robe and put it on him. Put a ring on his finger and sandals on his feet'" (Luke 15:22).

Jesus described a tax collector who humbly prayed for mercy in the temple and went home justified, or forgiven, because of his confession. "For all those who exalt themselves will be humbled, and those who humble themselves will be exalted" (Luke 18:14).

Following his denial of Jesus, Peter later affirmed his love for Christ and was reinstated to his ministry. "He [Peter] said, 'Lord, you know all things; you know that I love you'" (Jn. 21:17).

In Nehemiah's Day, upon hearing Ezra read from the Law of Moses, the people confessed their sins and those of their ancestors, leading to a renewed covenant with God. "Those of Israelite descent … stood in their places and confessed their sins and the sins of their ancestors" (Neh. 9:2).

The sinful woman who anointed Jesus' feet confessed her devotion to Jesus through her actions, and he declared her sins forgiven. "Then Jesus said to her, 'Your sins are forgiven'" (Luke 7:48).

Despite being a wicked king, Manasseh humbled himself and repented while in captivity. God heard his prayer and restored him. "And when he prayed to him, the Lord was moved by his entreaty and listened to his plea; so he brought him back to Jerusalem and to his kingdom. Then Manasseh knew that the Lord is God" (2 Ch. 33:13).

Many came to John the Baptist at the Jordan River to be baptized, confessing their sins as part of their repentance. "Confessing their sins, they were baptized by him in the Jordan River" (Matt. 3:6).

After witnessing God's power, many believers in Ephesus who had practiced sorcery confessed their deeds. "Many of those who believed now came and openly confessed what they had done … In this way the word of the Lord spread widely and grew in power" (Acts 19:18-20).

The thief crucified with Jesus confessed his guilt and asked Jesus to remember him, and Jesus promised him a place in Paradise. "We are punished justly, for we are getting what our deeds deserve. But this man [Jesus] has done nothing wrong" (Luke 23:41).

These examples demonstrate the biblical principle that: "Whoever conceals his transgressions will not prosper, but he who confesses and forsakes them will obtain mercy" (Prov. 28:13). For believers: "If we confess our sins, he is faithful and just to forgive us our sins and to cleanse us from all unrighteousness" (I Jn. 1:9).

Faith Unlocks the Door

This righteousness is given through faith in Jesus Christ ...

— Romans 3:22 —

Righteousness through faith (often called justification by faith) declares a person's righteousness before God not by their own deeds, but by trusting in God's promises and grace. In essence, we are credited with righteousness because of our faith.

Abraham is often considered the Father of Our Faith. He believed God's promise of a son in his old age, and it was attributed to him as righteousness. "Abram believed the Lord, and he credited it to him as righteousness" (Gen. 15:6).

By faith, Abel presented a sacrifice that was more

acceptable to God than his brother Cain's, and therefore he was praised as righteous. "By faith Abel offered to God a more acceptable sacrifice than Cain, through which he was commended as righteous" (Heb. 11:4).

King David described the blessedness of a man whom God considers righteous by faith alone, a truth he experienced himself after seeking God's mercy for his sins. "David ... speaks of the blessedness of the one to whom God credits righteousness apart from works ..." (Rom. 4:6).

In a corrupt world, Noah was a preacher of Godly living who became a recipient of faith-based righteousness when he obeyed God by building the ark. "By faith Noah ... became an heir of the righteousness that is in keeping with faith" (Heb. 11:7).

Despite her past as a prostitute, Rahab was justified because she believed the God of Israel was the true God and acted on that faith by protecting the spies. "By faith the prostitute Rahab ... was not killed with those who were disobedient" (Heb. 11:31).

In his final moments, the thief on the cross acknowledged his sin and expressed faith in Jesus' kingship, leading Jesus to declare him welcome in paradise. "'Jesus, remember me when you come into your kingdom' … Jesus answered him, 'Truly I tell you, today you will be with me in paradise'" (Luke 23:42-43).

The sinful woman in Luke 7 showed deep devotion to Jesus. He told her that her many sins were forgiven because of her faith. "Then he said to the woman, 'Your faith has saved you. Go in peace'" (Luke 7:50).

Paul explains that the gentiles, who did not follow Jewish law, attained righteousness through faith in Christ. "Gentiles, who did not pursue righteousness, have obtained it, a righteousness that is by faith" (Rom. 9:30).

Hebrews 11 lists many figures, including Enoch, Sarah, Isaac, and Joseph, who were acclaimed for their faith rather than their legal perfection. "These were all commended for their faith, yet none of them received what had been promised" (Heb. 11:39).

In the New Testament, every person who trusts in the words of Jesus is declared righteous as a gift. "This righteousness is given through faith in Jesus Christ to all who believe" (Rom. 3:22).

We can exhibit these levels of righteous faith

today by volunteering at a homeless shelter (Matt. 25); giving support for missions and providing for the needy (Prov. 22:9); befriending marginalized people to support God's inclusive love (1 Pet. 2:17); speaking truth about injustices or prosecuted believers (Josh. 1:9); admitting to our struggles and crediting God's amazing grace (Eph. 2:8-9); banishing worry for trust in God's provision (Phil. 4:6-7); offering help and understanding rather than criticism (Matt. 7:1-2); placing Bible study and worship before material accumulation (Matt. 6:33); volunteering to help neighbors or at our church (Gal. 5:6); and finally, we can avoid bad influences by choosing righteous people as our friends and mentors. When we seek out company with those who honor God, we will become righteous by association (Ps. 1).

Forgiveness Is a Person

I am the way and the truth and the life …

— John 14:6 —

Jesus is the exclusive path to God. Forgiveness

comes through him and no other. "I am the way, and the truth, and the life. No one comes to the Father except through me" (Jn. 14:6).

Paul writes that Jesus is the unique and only mediator between man and God. "For there is one God, and there is one mediator between God and men, the man Christ Jesus" (1 Tim. 2:5).

Peter declares that there is no name outside of Jesus that can provide our salvation. "And there is salvation in no one else, for there is no other name under heaven given among men by which we must be saved" (Acts 4:12).

Jesus is called "Mighty God, Everlasting Father, Prince of Peace" (Is. 9:6) and "Alpha and Omega, the first and the last" (Rev. 1:8). These are divine titles given to Jesus that are God's alone.

While angels refused worship, Jesus accepted that same worship as a divine figure. Read where the disciples worshipped him (Matt. 28:9) and all creation worships him while singing, "Worthy is the Lamb" (Rev. 5:12-13).

Jesus has all power over sin and death. Not only does he forgive sins (Mk. 2:5-7), he is the resurrection and the life (Jn. 11:25-26), and he conquers death.

Jesus is eternal from the beginning of time. John 1:1 states, "In the beginning was the Word, and the Word was with God, and the Word was God." Colossians 1:17 says he is before all things.

Old Testament prophecies, such as Isaiah 7:14 (Immanuel, God with us) and Micah 5:2 (ruler from Bethlehem), find their fulfillment in Jesus (Matt. 1:23).

"My Lord and My God!" Thomas's confession after seeing the resurrected Jesus (John 20:28) affirms Jesus' divinity.

John 3:16 highlights that God gave his Son, and that belief in him leads to eternal life, not death. Jesus is truly the only way to eternal life through salvation! "For God so loved the world that he gave his one and only Son, that whoever believes in him shall not perish but have eternal life."

Amen!

Receive and Rest

Now we who have believed enter that rest ...

— Hebrews 4:3 —

Finding rest and peace through salvation is central in our spiritual transformation. God offers us a deep, abiding sense of security in his presence. We see this illustrated throughout the Word.

Zacchaeus, the tax collector, was known for his dishonesty. Yet, he found immediate peace and a transformed heart after inviting Jesus into his home. "And Jesus said to him, 'Today salvation has come to this house …'" (Luke 19:9).

After a miraculous earthquake while Paul and Silas were in prison, the Philippian jailer was near despair. He asked how to be saved, and he and his household found immediate joy and peace through faith. "Believe in the Lord Jesus, and you will be saved—you and your household" (Acts 16:31).

The Samaritan woman at the well was burdened by social shame, yet she found living water and spiritual rest after an encounter with Jesus. She was so impacted by Jesus that she told her entire village about him, bringing them to believe in him. "Jesus answered her, 'If you knew the gift of God … he would have given you living water'" (Jn. 4:10).

The Ethiopian eunuch was traveling and

struggling to understand scripture. He found peace and went on his way with rejoicing after being baptized by Philip. "When they came up out of the water, the Spirit of the Lord suddenly took Philip away, and the eunuch did not see him again, but went on his way rejoicing" (Acts 8:39).

The woman who touched Jesus' cloak suffered from a chronic illness for twelve years. She found physical healing and internal peace through her faith in Christ's power. "He said to her, 'Daughter, your faith has healed you. Go in peace'" (Luke 8:48).

Unlike her sister Martha, who was anxious and troubled, Mary found rest by simply sitting at Jesus' feet to hear him speak. "But only one thing is necessary. Mary has chosen what is better, and it will not be taken away from her" (Luke 10:42).

Throughout his life of fleeing enemies, King David was able to set aside his worries by resting in God's salvation. "Truly my soul finds rest in God; my salvation comes from him" (Ps. 62:1).

After Elijah's victory over Ahab and the prophets of Jezebel, he was exhausted and fled for his life. Elijah found rest and restoration when God provided for his physical needs and spoke to him in a gentle whisper. "And after the fire came a gentle whisper … 'What are you doing here, Elijah?'" (1 Kings 19:12-13).

Jesus offers a universal invitation to find rest for all who labor and are heavy laden. He restores the soul through a relationship with him. "Come to me, all you who are weary and burdened, and I will give you rest" (Matt. 11:28).

Rest in God is interwoven with creation. From the beginnings of the world, God rested (Gen. 2:2-3). Resting on the Sabbath is for reflection and reconnection with God (Ex. 20:8-10). We learn through rest to rely on God's sovereignty rather than our self-effort (Ps. 37:70). We step aside from life's burdens and find inner calm (Ex. 33:14 and Matt. 11:28-30).

When we accept Jesus as our personal savior, we are surrounded by God's quietness and confidence. He is the Shepherd that leads us to peace and rest in him.

— 5 —

The Freedom to Forgive

Extending Grace to Others

Forgive as the Lord forgave you.

— Colossians 3:13 —

In Matthew 18:23-35, Jesus gives us the Parable of the Unforgiving Servant. The core of the story is that the servant is forgiven much, and yet he fails to offer the same forgiveness for a much smaller infraction.

How black are the sins which salvation wiped from our record? How grateful are we for the grace of

God? Are we willing to do for others what God has done for us?

This is a part of salvation. Salvation in and of itself is free, but along with our gift is the obligation that we must be equally generous and offer that same grace to those around us. Don't see this as a heavy burden. God is not trying to crimp your "style" or back you into a corner. Rather, salvation releases you to take the weight of what others have done to you and let Jesus carry that load. Let's look at how it's done.

Grace Given, Grace Extended

Freely you have received; freely give.

— Matthew 10:8 —

Grace is undeserved kindness, forgiveness, and restoration. When religious leaders demanded the woman caught in adultery be stoned, Jesus extended grace by refusing to condemn her and offering a path to transformation. "Jesus straightened up and asked her, 'Woman, where are they? Has no one condemned you?' 'No one, sir,' she said. 'Then neither do I condemn you,' Jesus declared. 'Go now and leave your life of sin'" (Jn. 8:10-11).

While on the cross, Jesus extended the ultimate grace to a criminal who acknowledged his sin, promising him eternal life. "Then he said, 'Jesus, remember me when you come into your kingdom.' Jesus answered him, 'Truly I tell you, today you will be with me in paradise'" (Luke 23:42-43).

After a sharp disagreement between Paul and Barnabas over John Mark's previous desertion, Barnabas extended grace by giving Mark a second chance at ministry. "They had such a sharp disagreement that they parted company. Barnabas took Mark and sailed for Cyprus, but Paul chose Silas and left, commended by the believers to the grace of the Lord" (Acts 15:39-40).

Despite Peter denying him three times, Jesus extended grace by appearing to him after the resurrection and restoring his leadership. "When they had finished eating, Jesus said to Simon Peter, 'Simon son of John, do you love me more than these?' 'Yes, Lord,' he said, 'you know that I love you.' Jesus said, 'Feed my lambs.'" (Jn. 21:15).

Joseph of Arimathea extended grace and honor by

providing his own new tomb for Jesus' burial, a high-stakes act of devotion. "Later, Joseph of Arimathea asked Pilate for the body of Jesus. Now Joseph was a disciple of Jesus, but secretly because he feared the Jewish leaders. With Pilate's permission, he came and took the body away" (John 19:38).

In one of Jesus' parables, a Samaritan extended grace to a Jewish man (historically an enemy) by providing life-saving care and resources. "But a Samaritan, as he traveled, came where the man was; and when he saw him, he took pity on him. He went to him and bandaged his wounds, pouring on oil and wine" (Luke 10:33-34).

While being martyred, Stephen extended grace to those killing him by praying for their forgiveness, echoing the example of Jesus on the cross. "Then he fell on his knees and cried out, 'Lord, do not hold this sin against them.' When he had said this, he fell asleep" (Acts 7:60).

Ananias extended grace to Saul (who would later be called Paul), a known persecutor of Christians, by visiting him, calling him "Brother," and assisting in his healing. "Then Ananias went to the house and entered it. Placing his hands on Saul, he said, 'Brother

Saul, the Lord—Jesus, who appeared to you on the road as you were coming here—has sent me so that you may see again and be filled with the Holy Spirit'" (Acts 9:17).

In the Parable of the Prodigal Son, the father extends grace to his wayward son by celebrating his return instead of demanding restitution or punishment. "But while he was still a long way off, his father saw him and was filled with compassion for him; he ran to his son, threw his arms around him and kissed him" (Luke 15:20).

Paul extended grace to a runaway slave, Onesimus, by advocating for his restoration as a "dear brother" rather than a criminal. "Perhaps the reason he was separated from you for a little while was that you might have him back forever—no longer as a slave, but better than a slave, as a dear brother" (Phil. 1:15-16).

As Christians, we can build habits of grace by replacing negative thoughts with a prayer for that person's well-being, intentionally looking for quiet ways to serve others, or if we fail to show grace, quickly apologizing and trying again.

Forgiveness Is Not Forgetting

*There is a time for everything, and a season
for every activity under the heavens:
[including] a time to heal ...*

— Ecclesiastes 3:1-3 —

The New Testament contains numerous examples and instructions regarding when to distance yourself from offenders for the sake of safety, peace, or spiritual integrity. We forgive them, but we don't let the one who has offended us remain in a position to do so again. These instances give us biblical foundations for setting healthy boundaries.

After preaching in Nazareth, his hometown, the crowd became enraged and attempted to throw Jesus off a cliff. Jesus passed through the crowd and left the hostile group of hecklers behind. "They got up, drove him out of the town, and took him to the brow of the hill on which the town was built, in order to throw him off the cliff. ³⁰ But he walked right through the crowd and went on his way" (Luke 4:29-30).

Again, aware that the Pharisees were conspiring

against him, Jesus chose to withdraw from the area rather than engage them. "But the Pharisees went out and plotted how they might kill Jesus. [15] Aware of this, Jesus withdrew from that place" (Matt. 12:14-15).

On a third occasion, Jesus instructed his disciples to symbolically distance themselves (shake the dust off their feet) from those who rejected their message. "If anyone will not welcome you or listen to your words, leave that home or town and shake the dust off your feet" (Matt. 10:14).

Following a healing in the region of the Gerasenes, the local people were fearful and asked Jesus to leave, and he complied. "Then all the people of the region of the Gerasenes asked Jesus to leave them, because they were overcome with fear. So he got into the boat and left" (Luke 8:37).

Paul and Barnabas separated after a sharp disagreement over whether to take John Mark on their journey. Their disagreement led to Paul and Barnabas choosing to part ways and continue their missions separately. "They had such a sharp disagreement that they parted company. Barnabas took Mark and sailed for Cyprus, [40] but Paul chose Silas and left, commended by the believers to the grace of the Lord"

(Acts 15:39-40).

Paul escaped Damascus to avoid the Jews plotting his death. When the plot against his life was uncovered, Paul left the city by being lowered in a basket through an opening in the wall. "But his followers took him by night and lowered him in a basket through an opening in the wall" (Acts 9:25).

Paul urged believers to identify and stay away from those who create divisions and obstacles to sound doctrine. "I urge you, brothers and sisters, to watch out for those who cause divisions and put obstacles in your way that are contrary to the teaching you have learned. Keep away from them" (Rom. 16:17).

Paul was more specific when he warned Timothy about Alexander the coppersmith, who had caused him harm and strongly opposed the gospel message. "Alexander the metalworker did me a great deal of harm. The Lord will repay him for what he has done. [15] You too should be on your guard against him, because he strongly opposed our message" (2 Tim. 4:14-15).

Paul instructed the church in Thessalonica to withdraw from members who were living in idleness and not following the teachings they had received. "Keep away from every believer who is idle and disruptive and does not live according to the teaching you received from us" (2 Thess. 3:6).

Jesus taught that when an offender refuses to listen to even spiritual leaders, treat them as an outsider and step away from the relationship. "If they still refuse to listen, tell it to the church; and if they refuse to listen even to the church, treat them as you would a pagan or a tax collector" (Matt. 18:17).

Forgiveness does not equate to being a doormat. We don't hold the offense against them, but we also don't forget so that it doesn't happen again.

Releasing the Offender

For if you forgive other people when they sin against you, your heavenly Father will also forgive you.

— Matthew 6:14 —

When someone offends us, we can reach out to crush them or restore them to a better place. At the least, we can release them from their guilt. Reena Virk of British Columbia, Canada, was murdered in 1997. Her mother, Suman, and her father met with and forgave Warren Glowatski, one of the men involved in their daughter's murder. Their act didn't change the facts, but it changed them when they released the murderer from his guilt.

Mari Johnson's parents were killed by a distracted trucker who was on his phone. The U.K. native worked toward forgiveness. Holding onto her anger was harming her, not him.

Paul Kohler, also of the U.K., was brutally attacked during a home invasion in 2014. Although the event was devastating, he met with one of his attackers and became a vocal supporter of restorative justice. Now, as a Member of Parliament (in 2024), he is pushing the U.K. legal system to provide more help to those who don't deserve it.

Jason Kasperek of Colorado endured a violent robbery in 1998. He met with Michael Clifton, one of his attackers, and now works with him to integrate ex-convicts back into society.

Mary Johnson of Minneapolis became an internationally recognized advocate for forgiveness. She forgave and worked with Oshea Israel, who murdered her son in 1993, to promote healing and reconciliation between victims and their offenders.

Nadine Collier was among the first to say, "I forgive you," following the 2015 shooting at Emanuel AME church.

Gabriel Horcasitas fatally shot Christopher Pelkey in a road rage incident. At his 2025 sentencing, Pelkey's sister, Stacey Wales, presented an AI video of her brother giving his killer a message of forgiveness.

In October of 2025, Marianne Alfonso Montes joined with church members to offer forgiveness to a shooter's family after an attack.

Also in 2025, Abdou Elly revealed his father met and extended forgiveness to the man who had killed his three children five years earlier.

Ah, you might say. This isn't the same as my offender. People don't know of my hurt. I've been hit in the core of my being, and my offender has twisted the knife. How can I release them? The pain is simply too much.

Let's look at these examples from the Bible:

Abigail took responsibility for her foolish husband, Nabal, in I Samuel 25:24. "She fell at his

[David's] feet and said: 'Pardon your servant, my lord, and let me speak to you; hear what your servant has to say.'"

Elisha healed Naaman, an enemy commander, in 2 Kings 5:14. "He went down and dipped himself in the Jordan seven times, as the man of God had told him, and his flesh was restored."

Stephen prayed for his killers as he was being stoned in Acts 7:60. "Then he fell on his knees and cried out, 'Lord, do not hold this sin against them.' When he had said this, he fell asleep."

David repeatedly spared Saul's life and refused to harm God's anointed in 1 Samuel 24:12. "And may the Lord avenge the wrongs you have done to me, but my hand will not touch you."

Joseph forgave his brothers for selling him into slavery in Genesis 45:8. "So then, it was not you who sent me here, but God."

And finally, the icing on the forgiveness cake: Jesus, while being crucified on the cross, prayed, "Father, forgive them, for they do not know what they are doing," in Luke 23:34.

How can we do less?

Breaking the Cycle of Bitterness

Get rid of all bitterness, rage and anger ...

— Ephesians 4:31 —

Christian living must be intentional. We cannot let it be an attachment to our "real" life, like a charm on a bracelet where we hold it up from time to time and show it off while saying, "See, this is my salvation charm. Isn't it pretty?" The book of Ephesians gives us a manual for how to go about imitating the life of Christ and living in holiness before God. We can't give ourselves over to sensuality. We must divorce ourselves from our old ways, always speak truthfully, and wash anger from the fabric of our day. No trash talking, no bitterness or rage, and above all, follow Jesus' example in kindness and compassion as we forgive those who have wronged us.

Only then can we break the cycle of bitterness.

In the Word we are told to forgive others as God has forgiven us in Christ (Eph. 4:32; Col. 3:13). This is central to our walk as a Christian.

We must also overcome evil with good, not by

fighting fire with fire. We replace one with the other (Rom. 12:21).

We don't turn to anger as our first response. We strive to be quick to listen, slow to speak, and unhurried to respond in anger (Jas. 1:19-20).

We refuse to strike out, either physically or verbally. God's Words says to remove bitterness, rage, anger, brawling, slander, and malice from your life (Eph. 4:31).

We pray for our enemies. Our goal is not to befriend them but to seek salvation and repentance for them rather than revenge. Jesus teaches us to love and pray for those who persecute us (Matt. 5:44).

We trust God to strengthen us and fill us with his Spirit. We can't change in our own power; we must ask God to be at our side (Gal. 5:16).

When we meditate on God's Word, his truth will saturate our hearts to overcome sinful behaviors (Heb. 4:12; 2 Cor. 3:18).

We can also reflect on the vastness of our own forgiveness from God, which helps us extend grace to others (Matt. 18).

Let's look at five practical steps you can begin to practice today.

Acknowledge your anger but refuse to let it fester into bitterness (Ps. 37:8).

Choose to be kind, compassionate, and forgiving, even when it's hard (Eph. 4:32).

Pray for those who hurt you, asking God to work in their lives and yours (Luke 6:28).

Let go of grudges and the desire for revenge, leaving vengeance to God (Rom. 12:19).

Seek God's presence, as bitterness cannot thrive where He dwells (Phil. 4:7).

Love Covers the Wound

Love covers a multitude of sins.

— I Peter 4:8 —

This verse is often taught as total forgiveness, no matter what someone does to us. Every day is fresh, and what was done to us yesterday doesn't matter.

That sounds good ... except when it leaves us in a vulnerable spot where our abuser feels comfortable taking advantage of us. So, let's break down this verse and look at it from the viewpoint of the early church.

"Agape love" is one that is selfish, sacrificial, and unconditional. So far, that matches what the modern church teaches, so we're on the mark there.

"Covers" comes from the Greek *kalupto*, which means to hide, veil, or bury. This word is also used in Proverbs 10:12 where the contrast is between stirring up conflicts or concealing hurts.

In the context of the 1st century church, Rome cast a dark shadow on the followers of Jesus. The early church could not afford to appear divided. "Covering" their sins meant keeping what happened in the church from being broadcast outside the church, i.e., no gossiping about what fellow believers were doing. Instead, offer your offender patience, charity, and understanding. Keep the wound within the church body as you work out your differences.

As Paul argued, time was short (1 Cor. 7:29), and the church's focus must be on maintaining forgiving relationships so that they could stand together in the coming trials.

Practical ways to see this verse is that we must not take offense at minor slights or irritations, and when we must deal with offenses, deal with them quietly and seek to restore the relationship rather than exposing the sin to "shame" our offender. When we absorb the cost of the relationship, whether in money, time, or emotions, rather than seek retaliation, we are emulating how Christ absorbed the weight of the offenses humanity piled on him.

Our love for our Christian brothers and sisters must act as a bridge that brings the sinner back to the covering of Christ's blood. As in a time of battle, we treat their wounds, bear the cost of their rehabilitation, and do it all with kindness. We are mirroring God and the ultimate covering he provided for all human sin through Christ's sacrifice.

When we feel wounded, love covers the wound by veiling or burying the offense. When we uncover the wound and expose it to critique by the world, we are slipping into hate (Prov. 10:12).

The Bible uses the phrase "love covers sin" to illustrate how grace, forgiveness, and godly affection can mend broken relationships and provide spiritual healing. The following set of verses is central to reconciliation and Christian fellowship.

"Above all, love each other deeply, because love covers over a multitude of sins" (1 Pet. 4:8). This reference suggests a love that is stretched to cover or contain, similar to an athlete's focus that ignores everything not beneficial to winning. We must prioritize forgiveness over holding grudges.

"Hatred stirs up conflict, but love covers over all wrongs" (Prov. 10:12). Here we establish a clear contrast. While hatred actively searches for faults to cause division, love works to minimize and reconcile those same offenses to maintain peace.

"Whoever turns a sinner from the error of their way will save them from death and cover over a multitude of sins" (Jas. 5:20). The act of love is shown through helping a fellow believer return to the right path. We effectively cover their sins by bringing them into God's grace and forgiveness.

"Whoever covers an offense seeks love, but he who repeats a matter separates close friends" (Prov. 17:9). Constantly bringing up someone's past mistakes is an act of division, whereas choosing not to gossip about or dwell on a wrong is a pursuit of love.

"Through steadfast love and faithfulness iniquity is atoned for; through the fear of the Lord a person avoids evil" (Prov. 16:6). Covering another's sins points to our deep relationship with God. Our love directs them away from sin and toward mercy.

— 6 —

Forgiven for a Purpose

Living in Your New Identity

You are a chosen people ... that you may declare the praises of him.

— I Peter 2:9 —

Now that you're forgiven, what's next? What's the arrow that points you down life's road and to your eternal destination? You are, after all, on a new spiritual journey. Yours is a walk of sanctification as you endeavor to become more like Jesus.

How do you do that?

Jesus lived righteously, served God rather than expecting people to cater to him, did good works for others, and exhibited the fruit of the Spirit as he shared his message with humanity. He glorified his Father in all things and was worthy to be called the Son of God.

There are several ways we can emulate Jesus as we search to find his purpose in our life. We can join a church and engage in fellowship, teaching, and worship with other like-minded believers. The Bible should be core to our studies as we seek to understand God's instructions for our life. When we communicate with God in prayer and ask for his guidance, we will receive instructions to apply God's commands to all areas of our life, including relationships, finances, and more.

When we live righteously, we deny ungodliness and live a faith-filled, loving life, enabling us to embrace our new identity and let go of our past guilt, while rejoicing that we are a new creation in Christ.

You Are Not What You Did

As far as the east is from the west,

so far has he removed our transgressions from us.

— Psalm 103:12 —

Your repentance through a direct encounter with Jesus ignites a transformation from the old you to a spiritually transformed child of God. The Word gives us multiple examples of the life-changing effects of our encounter with the Savior of the world. Who we once were and what we once did are no longer of any account in the eyes of God. We have become brand new through God's redemptive power.

Paul (Saul of Tarsus) was a Pharisee who oversaw the stoning of Stephen. He was out to bring the newly formed church to its knees. After a blinding encounter with Jesus on the road to Damascus, he became one of the primary drivers of the church and wrote much of the New Testament. (Acts 9:1-22)

Peter, also known as Simon, was a self-motivated and impulsive follower of Jesus. He famously denied knowing Jesus three times. After repenting, he was restored by Jesus and became a leader of the early church. (Jn. 21:15-19; Acts 2)

Zacchaeus, a wealthy and often corrupt chief tax collector, was despised by his community. After meeting Jesus, he repented of his greed and promised to give half his possessions to the poor and repay those he cheated fourfold. (Luke 19:1-10)

Mary Magdalene was plagued by seven demons until Jesus delivered her. Following her transformation, she became Jesus' supporter and disciple and was the first person to see Jesus after his resurrection. (Luke 8:1-3; Jn. 20:11-18)

King David was a man after God's heart. When he committed adultery with Bathsheba and orchestrated the murder of her husband, he was confronted by the prophet Nathan. David repented and was forgiven. (2 Sam. 11-12; Ps. 51)

Jonah fled from God's command to preach to Nineveh, and God allowed him to be swallowed by a great fish. Inside the fish, he repented. His subsequent ministry to Nineveh led to the repentance of an entire city. (Jon. 1-3)

Rahab was a prostitute living in Jericho. She trusted in God and hid two Israelite spies. Although the people she had lived among for her entire life died, she was spared during Jericho's destruction and became an ancestor of Jesus. (Josh. 2; Jas. 2:25)

The thief on the cross recognized Jesus' innocence, confessed his guilt, and asked Jesus to remember him. Jesus gave him a promise of paradise. (Luke 23:39-43)

Moses became a fugitive after murdering an Egyptian taskmaster. God later called him to return and lead the Israelites out of slavery. Moses was transformed from a murderer to the leader of a nation. (Ex. 2-3)

How bad is your past? What are the skeletons in your closet? Anger? Vengeance? *Murder?* In the natural world, what we do has a price. Our choices come back to haunt us, whether in our finances, health, or relationships. King David's child with Bathsheba died. The thief on the cross suffered painfully. Moses spent years in the wilderness and wasn't allowed to enter the Promised Land. Yet, each of these people was sanctified in the sight of God and moved forward into greater things. Once you accept salvation and the forgiveness of Christ, you become new in him.

God has amazing plans for your future!

Walking in Worthiness

Live a life worthy of the calling you have received.

— Ephesians 4:1 —

Walking in worthiness describes a life of godly character, moral courage, and persistent faithfulness to God's calling on our lives. We can look to the Bible for multiple examples of historical figures that show us how it's done. When we model our attitudes and behaviors on them, we can trust we are on God's path toward sanctification and pure living.

Enoch "walked faithfully with God" in such a close daily fellowship that God took him directly to heaven without him experiencing death. "Enoch walked faithfully with God; then he was no more, because God took him away" (Gen. 5:24).

Noah lived in a generation of widespread corruption, yet he remained blameless and spent over a century building the ark by faith in things not yet seen. "Noah was a righteous man, blameless among the people of his time, and he walked faithfully with

God" (Gen. 6:9).

Abraham is known as the Father of Faith. He left his homeland at age 75 without a destination, trusting in God's promise for his future. "By faith Abraham, when called to go to a place he would later receive as his inheritance, obeyed and went, even though he did not know where he was going" (Heb. 11:8).

Joseph, the favorite son of Jacob, remained faithful to God's calling after being sold into slavery by his brothers, eventually rising to save his family and Egypt from famine. "You intended to harm me, but God intended it for good to accomplish what is now being done, the saving of many lives" (Gen. 50:20).

Moses was reluctant and considered himself "slow of speech," yet he became a powerful leader who confronted Pharaoh to lead the Israelites out of Egyptian slavery. "By faith he left Egypt, not fearing the king's anger; he persevered because he saw him who is invisible" (Heb. 11:27).

Ruth, a widow and foreigner, chose loyalty to her mother-in-law and to the God of Israel over her own security, ultimately becoming part of the lineage of Jesus. "Where you go I will go, and where you stay I will stay. Your people will be my people and your

God my God" (Ruth 1:16).

David was described as a "man after God's own heart." He served his generation as a shepherd, warrior, and king, always returning to God in repentance. "I have found David son of Jesse, a man after my own heart; he will do everything I want him to do" (Acts 13:22).

Esther risked her life to fulfill her calling as queen, intervening to save her people from extermination during a time of great danger. "And who knows but that you have come to your royal position for such a time as this?" (Est. 4:14).

Daniel maintained a life of disciplined prayer and integrity while serving in high-ranking positions under pagan kings, even in the face of death. "Now when Daniel learned that the decree had been published … three times a day he got down on his knees and prayed, giving thanks to his God" (Dan. 6:10).

The Apostle Paul had a life-changing encounter with Christ, after which he lived "a life worthy of the calling" by enduring extreme suffering to spread the gospel. "I press on toward the goal to win the prize for which God has called me heavenward in Christ Jesus" (Phil. 3:14).

A worthy walk with Christ doesn't mean perfection. We can look back at each of these people, and often, they stumbled. Their worthiness to their calling came in getting back up, repenting of their mistakes, and matching footsteps with God. We do it one day at a time.

Ambassadors of Grace

We are therefore Christ's ambassadors ...

— 2 Corinthians 5:20 —

Many modern Christians serve as ambassadors of grace, a term that describes individuals representing Christ's message through radical forgiveness, compassion, and service. These are ordinary people who have earned a place as modern examples of Christians whose stories reflect the example of Christ.

Bob Goff is a "recovering lawyer" and founder of the nonprofit Love Does. Goff is known for his radical accessibility and whimsical approach to faith. His story centers on living out his faith through simple, persistent acts of love, such as including his personal cell phone number in his books to encourage strangers; and founding schools for children in conflict zones like Afghanistan and Uganda.

Corrie ten Boom claimed her primary fame during WWII, but her modern legacy is defined by her post-war ministry of reconciliation. Her most famous story of grace involves meeting and forgiving a former Nazi guard from the concentration camp where her family died, a moment she described as an act of God's grace working through her when her own strength failed.

John Mark Comer is a former megachurch pastor turned author and teacher. Comer advocates for a slower way of life that prioritizes a strong spiritual foundation over modern hustle and bustle. His story emphasizes grace as the power to change our internal character and navigate disillusionment and stress with a peace-focused, Christ-centered perspective.

Becca Stevens, the founder of Thistle Farms, has dedicated her life to helping women survivors of trafficking, prostitution, and addiction. Her ministry operates on the principle that love heals, offering grace in the form of long-term housing, employment, and a community that does not judge survivors for their past.

Mike Lindell is known publicly for his business, but he often shares his personal testimony of overcoming severe crack cocaine addiction through his faith. He uses his platform as an example of transformative grace, testifying that no matter how far someone has fallen, God's grace offers a path to complete restoration and new purpose.

At the start of 2026, Pope Leo XIV used his platform to issue powerful calls for global reconciliation and non-violence. His message focuses on "disarming our hearts," while he urges believers to act as ambassadors by rejecting defensive or violent rhetoric in favor of grace-filled dialogue and peacebuilding.

Bryan Stevenson is recognized for his legal work with the Equal Justice Initiative. His story is deeply rooted in his Christian faith and the concept of "just mercy." He serves as an ambassador of grace by representing those on death row and advocating for the poor, operating on the belief that each of us is more than the worst thing we've ever done.

When we look for ways to show grace to the people around us, whether in small or great ways, we act as the hand of Jesus and change lives.

A Life that Reflects Mercy

Act justly, love mercy, and walk humbly ...

— Micah 6:8 —

In the Bible, mercy is God's compassionate, forgiving, and undeserved kindness. In his mercy, he often sets aside punishment and offers the needy healing, provision, and companionship (Ex. 34:6-7; Matt. 9:13; Luke 6:36). God's nature is expressed through acts of compassion and kindness, and we are called to extend this same merciful treatment to others.

We might better understand mercy as the compassionate treatment of those in distress, particularly when it is within our power to punish or harm them. It is a foundational attribute of God's character and a central requirement for the life of a believer.

Mercy is often contrasted with justice. Justice is getting what you deserve, while mercy is not getting the punishment you deserve. We withhold our offender's deserved punishment for something kinder, especially for those who are miserable, afflicted, or needy. Showing compassion for the helpless is core to the biblical meaning of mercy.

We must also show forgiveness as part of mercy. Mercy is inextricably linked to God's willingness to forgive sins and restore broken relationships. We must be willing to live out God's gift to us through the mercy we show to others.

The biblical definition of mercy is enhanced by looking back to the original languages of Hebrew and Greek which reveal several vital nuances.

Chesed in the Hebrew can be translated as "steadfast love" or "lovingkindness." This represents God's loyal, covenant-based mercy. He has brokered a deal with us, one that cannot be broken.

Rachamim in the Hebrew is derived from the word for womb, *rechem*. Imagine the deep, visceral, maternal compassion a mother has for her new-born child.

Eleos in the Greek is the most common New Testament term for mercy. It suggests showing pity or kindness toward those in need.

In Exodus 34:6, God defines himself as "merciful and gracious, slow to anger, and abounding in steadfast love." That sets a high bar for us. During Jesus' ministry he was the ultimate "face of mercy." He healed the sick, comforted the grieving, and pardoned those who persecuted him.

We are instructed to love mercy (Mic. 6:8) and to be merciful, just as our Father is merciful (Luke 6:36). The Beatitudes also state that those who are merciful will receive mercy (Matt. 5:7).

The parable of the Good Samaritan illustrates mercy as a practical, boundary-crossing action to help someone in distress (Luke 10:25-37).

The crucifixion is viewed as the supreme act of mercy, where God placed the punishment for sin on Jesus so that believers could receive forgiveness.

We must be all-in on this. It is a biblical directive that we cannot afford to set aside.

From Scar to Story

*They overcame by the blood of the Lamb
and the word of their testimony.*

— Revelation 12:11 —

Biblical scholars and theologians highlight the theme of suffering for Christ as central to the early

Christian experience. We shudder at believers who were fed to wild animals in the Coliseum.

It still happens today. Modern missionaries are beaten or even killed for their faith.

In Haiti in May of 2024, American missionaries David and Natalie Lloyd, along with Haitian director Jude Montes, were killed by armed gangs in Port-au-Prince. Despite the country's extreme violence, they had chosen to continue their humanitarian and spiritual work. The group was ambushed while leaving a church youth group.

On North Sentinel Island, in November of 2018, John Allen Chau, an American evangelical missionary, was killed by the Sentinelese, a tribe living in voluntary isolation in the Andaman Islands. Chau was attempting to introduce the tribe to Christianity despite legal prohibitions against visiting the island.

In the Democratic Republic of the Congo during 2024-2025, Islamist groups like the ADF targeted Christian villages, leading to the abduction and killing of hundreds of believers who refused to recant their faith. These believers now carry physical scars or have endured significant bodily suffering due to their devotion to Jesus.

In the Bible, Jesus Christ is the number one example of bearing scars for humanity. He rose from the dead with visible wounds in his hands and side from the crucifixion. "Reach out your hand and put it into my side. Stop doubting and believe" (Jn. 20:27).

Paul the Apostle famously stated he bore the marks of Jesus in his body, likely referring to scars from being flogged five times, beaten with rods three times, and once stoned. "From now on, let no one cause me trouble, for I bear on my body the marks of Jesus" (Gal. 6:17).

Peter, along with other apostles, was arrested and flogged for preaching about Jesus' resurrection, leaving physical marks of his commitment. "They called the apostles in and had them flogged … The apostles left … rejoicing because they had been counted worthy of suffering disgrace for the Name" (Acts 5:40-41).

Stephen is recognized as the first Christian martyr. He was physically battered by stones until he died for his testimony about Christ. "While they were stoning him, Stephen prayed, 'Lord Jesus, receive my spirit'" (Acts 7:59).

While accompanying Paul, Silas was severely

flogged and imprisoned in Philippi for his ministry. "After they had been severely flogged, they were thrown into prison … they were praying and singing hymns to God" (Acts 16:23-25).

Thomas is traditionally believed to have been speared to death in India. He represents the many disciples who suffered physical trauma for their global mission. "Then Thomas … said to the rest of the disciples, 'Let us also go, that we may die with him'" (Jn. 11:16).

James, the brother of John, was the first of the twelve apostles to be executed for his faith, specifically killed with a sword by King Herod. "It was about this time that King Herod Agrippa … had James, the brother of John, put to death with the sword" (Acts 12:1-2).

Bartholomew, a.k.a. Nathanael, was brutally martyred—specifically skinned alive—for refusing to renounce his faith in Jesus, according to early church history and tradition. "Nathanael answered … 'Rabbi, you are the Son of God; you are the king of Israel'" (Jn. 1:49).

Antipas is mentioned by name in the Book of Revelation. He was a faithful witness who was killed in the city of Pergamum for his devotion. "Yet you remain true to my name … even in the days of Antipas, my faithful witness, who was put to death in your city" (Rev. 2:13).

John the Apostle was exiled to the island of Patmos and reportedly suffered other physical persecutions, such as being boiled in oil before his exile, according to early Christian writer Tertullian. "I, John … was on the island of Patmos because of the word of God and the testimony of Jesus" (Rev. 1:9).

Our scars might be visible or invisible. PTSD is a thing, even if we haven't spent time on a battlefield during wartime. Our scars serve as our story of our faith in the overcoming blood of the Lamb and our redemption through Jesus Christ.

— 7 —

The Journey Continues

Living Daily in Forgiveness

His mercies are new every morning.

— Lamentations 3:23 —

Forgiveness is a daily thing, one that is three-pronged. To live each day in God's grace, we must forgive others as God has forgiven us, release any bitterness from any wrongs done to us, and pray for a daily pardon from sin.

These are crucial for maintaining fellowship with God and receiving his continued forgiveness. As we work toward sanctification, we continually put off our old man and the world in which we live, and we take on the new man who lives in daily forgiveness and communion with God. "You were taught, with regard to your former way of life, to put off your old self, which is being corrupted by its deceitful desires" (Eph. 4:22).

Five key biblical principles for living in daily forgiveness are to be kind, tenderhearted, and forgiving to others as Christ is to us (Col. 3:23). We must also understand that our forgiveness from God is directly linked to us forgiving others (Mk. 11:25). We must daily seek and grant forgiveness, both from God and people (Matt. 6:12). We cannot let anger, rage, or bitterness come between us and the peace of God (Eph. 4:31-32), and we should practice forgiving repeatedly and without limit (Luke 17:3-4).

Daily Grace for Daily Struggles

My grace is sufficient for you ...

— 2 Corinthians 12:9 —

Claiming daily grace involves actively relying on God's unmerited favor through intentional habits and mindsets. This is a choice, one that we make each hour of the day, from the time we climb out of bed to the last thing we do at night. If we pray, "God give me your grace for the day," and then go on with our day while we ignore God, we've lost the point and will become mired in our old man, while our new man becomes increasingly distant. Here are thirteen actionable ways to walk in grace:

Begin with morning prayer. Commit your day to God immediately upon waking to build a strong, regular communication with him. "In the morning, Lord, you hear my voice; in the morning I lay my requests before you and wait expectantly" (Ps. 5:3).

Regularly expose your heart to the Word of God to find direction, comfort, and transformation. Your daily Bible intake will strengthen your relationship with him. "Man shall not live by bread alone, but by every word that proceeds out of the mouth of God" (Matt. 4:4).

Rest in God's sufficiency. When fighting with self and sin, instead of relying on your own strength, allow God's grace to empower you in difficult moments.

"My grace is sufficient for you, for my power is made perfect in weakness" (2 Cor. 12:9).

Practice quick and full forgiveness. Release the weight of unforgiveness on an ongoing basis, just as you were forgiven by Christ. "Be kind and compassionate to one another, forgiving each other, just as in Christ God forgave you" (Eph. 4:32).

Choose to be humble. Recognize your complete dependence on God and receive a fresh supply of his favor. "God opposes the proud but shows favor to the humble" (1 Pet. 5:5; Jas. 4:6).

Be content in all circumstances. Choose to be satisfied with what God has provided, whether you feel blessed or stressed. "I have learned to be content whatever the circumstances" (Phil. 4:11).

Use prayer not as a last resort, but as a first response to both big dreams and tiny frustrations. "Pray without ceasing" (1 Thess. 5:17).

Live one day at a time. Yesterday is "in the can" and the stage has been struck. Tomorrow's script hasn't arrived. Guard against anxiety by trusting God for "daily manna" rather than worrying about future problems. The only stage you are on is today. "Therefore do not worry about tomorrow, for tomorrow will worry about itself" (Matt. 6:34).

Serve others with your spiritual gifts. Are you a musician? Then sign up to sing. Is childcare your thing? Then volunteer on Sunday mornings. View your talents as forms of God's grace meant to be shared with the community. "Each of you should use whatever gift you have received to serve others, as faithful stewards of God's grace" (1 Pet. 4:10).

Actively look for small blessings throughout the day and give God the glory. Practicing daily gratitude will change your outlook on your life. "Give thanks in all circumstances; for this is God's will for you in Christ Jesus" (1 Thess. 5:18).

When you stumble, do not hide. Approach God with confidence. Draw near to the throne of grace to receive mercy and a fresh start. "Let us then approach God's throne of grace with confidence, so that we may receive mercy and find grace to help us in our time of need" (Heb. 4:16).

Observe a regular sabbath rest time. It doesn't have to be on a Sunday. Prioritize your day to honor your Creator and acknowledge that you are a new person in him. "Remember the Sabbath day by keeping it holy" (Ex. 20:8).

Focus on progress, not perfection. Accept that you will make mistakes and trust that God is still working on you. "I press on toward the goal to win the prize for which God has called me heavenward in Christ Jesus" (Phil. 3:14).

Learning to Live Free

You were called to be free …

— Galatians 5:13 —

The forgiveness that comes through salvation offers the modern Christian freedom in many aspects of life. The first and most obvious is freedom from guilt and shame, as expressed in 1 John 1:9. "If we confess our sins, he is faithful and just and will forgive us our sins and purify us from all unrighteousness." Our slate is wiped clean. The mud is washed away. God no longer sees the muck that used to cling so tightly to us.

Condemnation is also banished. God holds out his hand and draws us to him. Romans 8:1 says that through God's forgiveness, we are purified in him.

"Therefore, there is now no condemnation for those who are in Christ Jesus."

Romans 6:14 tells us that the chains of sin no longer control our thoughts, emotions, and lives. "For sin shall no longer be your master, because you are not under the law, but under grace." This also relieves us from the fear of death. "That by his death he might break the power of him who holds the power of death—that is, the devil— [15] and free those who all their lives were held in slavery by their fear of death" (Heb. 2:14-15).

We can kick aside religious dogma and manmade rules for salvation. Religious legalism no longer applies to us. "It is for freedom that Christ has set us free. Stand firm, then, and do not let yourselves be burdened again by a yoke of slavery" (Gal. 5:1).

We are now free to approach God with freedom from anxiety and worry, so that we can live out God's purpose in our lives. "Through faith in him we may approach God with freedom and confidence" (Eph. 3:12) and "by prayer and petition, with thanksgiving, present your requests to God" (Phil. 4:6), "for we are God's handiwork, created in Christ Jesus to do good works, which God prepared in advance for us to do"

(Eph. 2:10).

We can now claim our rights as a child of God through Galatians 4:7. "You are no longer a slave, but God's child; and since you are his child, God has made you also an heir." As God's heir, we live free from Satan's dominion. "He has rescued us from the dominion of darkness and brought us into the kingdom of the Son he loves" (Col. 1:13).

When we truly know the security of living as a member of God's family, the empty love of the world no longer haunts us. We no longer look for the "reason" we are being loved, and in turn, we become infused with the freedom to authentically love others, found in I John 4:7. "Let us love one another, for love comes from God. Everyone who loves has been born of God and knows God." Dark thoughts and second-guessing no longer haunt us as we live mentally free from our past. "Now the Lord is the Spirit, and where the Spirit of the Lord is, there is freedom" (2 Cor. 3:17). Fear and torment are no longer part of our days. "There is no fear in love. But perfect love drives out fear, because fear has to do with punishment" (I Jn. 4:18).

Through the forgiveness of Christ, we become free

from the world's empty values. The partying … the drive to earn more, to have more and to one-up our neighbors … is part of the old man. We are new in Christ. "If the Son sets you free, you will be free indeed" (Jn. 8:36). Our freedom in Christ gives us the choice to live a life that benefits those around us and leads to an eternal relationship with the Father. "But now that you have been set free from sin and have become slaves of God, the benefit you reap leads to holiness, and the result is eternal life" (Rom. 6:22).

The Role of Repentance

Repent and turn to God, so that your sins may be wiped out …

— Acts 3:19 —

Repentance is more than just feeling sorry. It is a transformative about-face from sin toward God, and it changes every part of who we are and how we live. Not only does repentance allow God to cleanse us spiritually, but it also showers us with benefits that flow directly from the throne of God. It begins with triggering God's promise to wipe away past wrongs and purify the soul. "Repent, then, and turn to God, so that your sins may be wiped out ..." (Acts 3:19).

After being confronted for his sin with Bathsheba, King David repented, and God removed his guilt (Ps. 32:5). David still had to deal with the consequences of what he'd done, but he was spiritually restored before God.

Turning to God also brings a deep sense of renewal and breathing room for the spirit, a type of spiritual time out and renewal. "Repent, then, and turn to God, so that your sins may be wiped out, that times of refreshing may come from the Lord" (Acts 3:19). If you are burdened by a heavy load of secret sin, you will receive sudden peace and lightness after confessing it to God.

Repentance restores our relationship with God and removes the barrier of sin that prevents our prayers from reaching the throne, allowing for intimate fellowship and a return to the Father. "Return to me, and I will return to you, says the Lord Almighty" (Mal. 3:7). We see this in the example of the prodigal son, who was restored to his father's house and status immediately upon his humble return

(Luke 15:20-24).

Sincere repentance can stay God's hand of judgment against an individual or a community, even when the world thinks the judgment is deserved. "But unless you repent, you too will all perish" (Luke 13:3). The story of Jonah and the miraculous repentance that swept over the city of Nineveh as they were spared from total destruction is one for the history books (Jon. 3:10).

Our repentance also triggers heavenly rejoicing in the spiritual realm. We can read of this unique benefit in Luke 15:7. "There will be more rejoicing in heaven over one sinner who repents than over ninety-nine righteous persons who do not need to repent." The parable of the Lost Sheep illustrates the Shepherd's (God's) immense joy when what was lost is found through repentance (Luke 15:4-7).

God offers deliverance and protection from the enemy for those who come to repentance. He closes the door to demonic footholds by realigning us with his authority. "Submit yourselves, then, to God. Resist the devil, and he will flee from you" (Jas. 4:7). When Israel cried out in repentance, God raised up deliverers to free them from their oppressors (Jud.

2:16-19).

The act of acknowledging our sin through our act of repentance naturally crushes pride and fosters a teachable spirit. "God opposes the proud but shows favor to the humble" (Jas. 4:6). When Zacchaeus the tax collector humbled himself before Jesus, it led to a radical change from greed to extreme generosity (Luke 19:8).

Our next benefit isn't always a direct "repent and be healed" benefit, but when we relieve the stress of sin on our mind and body, we receive restored health and vitality. "Confess your sins to each other and pray for each other so that you may be healed" (Jas. 5:16). In Isaiah 38:1-5, we find where King Hezekiah repented and wept before God, who then healed his terminal illness and added fifteen years to his life.

Repentance often provides access to spiritual wisdom, as it clears our mind to receive divine instruction. "God will grant them repentance leading them to a knowledge of the truth" (2 Tim. 2:25). After the Apostle Paul's conversion and repentance, his spiritual blindness was removed, allowing him to understand the Scriptures in a new light (Acts 9).

The repentance of the thief on the cross illustrates

our assurance of eternal life. Jesus immediately promised him entry into Paradise (Luke 23:41-43). The thief's repentance exposes the entry point into the Kingdom of God and the promise of salvation. "Godly sorrow brings repentance that leads to salvation and leaves no regret" (2 Cor. 7:10).

Guarding the Heart

Above all else, guard your heart, for everything you do flows from it.

— Proverbs 4:23 —

Guarding the heart remains a central mandate for Christians, as the heart is considered the wellspring of life. We must move past hoping for the best as we hit the button on our remote to watch yet another episode of "Days of Our Lives" or "The Jerry Springer Show." I want to give you thirteen practical ways to guard your heart against sin.

First is the simple one you've already begun. Even the unchurched know the shortest verse in the Bible ("Jesus wept.") and the salvation scripture found in

John 3:16. Memorize verses specifically targeting your frequent temptations to use as a spiritual shield when they arise. "I have hidden your word in my heart that I might not sin against you" (Ps. 119:11).

When a negative or lustful thought enters your mind, immediately replace it with a word of truth or a prayer. Take your thoughts captive with intentional movements toward God. "We take captive every thought to make it obedient to Christ" (2 Cor. 10:5).

Saturate your mind with truth. Intentionally choose godly media, books, or music that strengthen your faith rather than worldly content. "Whatever is true … noble … right … pure … lovely … admirable—if anything is excellent or praiseworthy—think about such things" (Phil. 4:8).

Begin and end each day by asking the Holy Spirit to specifically guard your mind and soul from the day's potential snares. "And lead us not into temptation, but deliver us from evil" (Matt. 6:13). Then filter your relationships throughout the day. Surround yourself with people immersed in God who will encourage your walk with Christ rather than trigger sinful habits. "Do not be misled: 'Bad company corrupts good character'" (1 Cor. 15:33).

Quit walking the worldly tightrope of greed or envy. If you struggle with overspending, do not browse online shops when you are bored or alone. "Clothe yourselves with the Lord Jesus Christ, and do not think about how to gratify the desires of the flesh" (Rom. 13:14). You can also follow Joseph's example by physically leaving a situation immediately when it turns toward sin, rather than trying to test your willpower. In other words, flee temptation immediately. Get your bones out of there as if the floor is lava. "Flee youthful passions and pursue righteousness" (2 Tim. 2:22).

One way to establish healthy boundaries is by setting software filters on your devices or creating rules about who you spend time with alone to protect your integrity. "I made a covenant with my eyes not to look lustfully at a young woman" (Job 31:1). Invite a trusted mentor or friend into your "heart-guarding process" to help identify blind spots you may miss. When you seek accountability, you create a barrier against sin. "Therefore confess your sins to each other and pray for each other so that you may be healed" (Jas. 5:16).

When social hiccups happen (as they inevitably

will), forgive quickly to prevent bitterness and hatred from taking root and poisoning your heart. When you resolve conflicts in a timely manner, you "do not give the devil a foothold" (Eph. 4:27). Stay focused on your God-given calling and goals to keep your mind from wandering into sinful fantasies or unproductive habits. Ask God to open doors and then step through to seize his opportunity. Stay rooted in his purpose for your life. "Idle hands are the devil's workshop" (Prov. 16:27, para.).

Resist sin by submitting to God. That means, when tempted, first verbally acknowledge God's authority over you, then tell the temptation no in the name of Jesus. "Submit yourselves therefore to God. Resist the devil, and he will flee from you" (Jas. 4:7). Finally, acknowledge your human weakness and actively draw near to the throne of grace. God will give you mercy and power that exceeds your own willpower. You can rely on the Holy Spirit's strength. "I can do all things through Christ who strengthens me" (Phil. 4:13).

Running the Race with Confidence

Let us run with perseverance the race marked out for us.

— Hebrews 12:1 —

Confidence in salvation allows a Christian to follow Christ from a position of security and love. We can step out boldly, supported by a sincere, deep relationship with God and support from our Christian community. Our walk with Christ will bleed into our workplace, our family relationships, and our interactions with the cashier at the local mart. We will become the hand of Jesus to those in need, and the face of God to those who are hurting.

The hardest part of running our race with confidence is placing our trust in Christ's sacrifice, not in our human effort. We can't earn our salvation, only receive it. "Jesus said, 'It is finished.' With that, he bowed his head and gave up his spirit" (Jn. 19:30). We can rest on the knowledge that our sin debt is paid in full.

Rather than rely on us, we must rely on God's personal promises. Our confidence comes from God's truthfulness and promises to save believers. "I write these things to you who believe in the name of the Son of God so that you may know that you have eternal life" (I Jn. 5:13). We can trust the Bible as our guarantee of salvation.

In the quiet times, we must listen for the witness of the Holy Spirit. The Holy Spirit confirms a believer's status as a child of God. "The Spirit himself testifies with our spirit that we are God's children" (Rom. 8:16). We will experience inner peace when we call out to God as our spiritual Father.

A new life with new desires shows Christ is working within us. As we choose right actions and find sin less appealing, we gain confidence in our salvation. "Therefore, if anyone is in Christ, the new creation has come: The old has gone, the new is here!" (2 Cor. 5:17). The evidence of a changed life is proof of our sonship in the family of God.

A willingness to follow God's commands is a mark of a true believer. We can practice conscious obedience to scripture by intentionally living by biblical principles. "We know that we have come to know him if we keep his commands" (I Jn. 2:3).

Sacrificial love for other believers indicates we have made a spiritual transition from death to life through repentance. "We know that we have passed from death to life, because we love each other" (I Jn. 3:14). We prove our sacrificial love when we help fellow church members in need even when it puts us in a position of discomfort.

Sorrow when we stumble (trust me, we will) and desiring restored fellowship with Christ and our fellow believers helps us maintain a deep awareness of sin. True believers are saddened by sin because it disappoints God. "If we claim to be without sin, we deceive ourselves and the truth is not in us" (I Jn. 1:8).

A desire for sound doctrine through seeking in-depth Bible teaching shows a heart that is born again. When we cultivate a hunger for God's Word, we draw closer to him. "Crave pure spiritual milk, so that by it you may grow up in your salvation" (I Pet. 2:2).

We find hope in difficult times by focusing on eternity with Christ. Looking forward to Christ's return helps purify a believer's life. We can refocus from our earthly existence to the awesomeness of our coming hope. "What we will be has not yet been made known. But we know that when Christ appears, we shall be like him, for we shall see him as he is"

(1 Jn. 3:2).

Finally, we find hope in God's power to persevere. We place our confidence in God's ability to complete the work he started in us at the time of our salvation. We stand on our belief that God will not abandon us. "Being confident of this, that he who began a good work in you will carry it on to completion until the day of Christ Jesus" (Phil. 1:6).

Our walk with Christ is often described as a narrow path, a way of life, or walking in the light. It is also a race with a prize at the end. You can achieve the prize through embracing the power of God's forgiveness to transform your life. His grace is unshakable, and he desires to offer it to you.

You've finished *Grace Unshakable!*

Congratulations!

God can and will break your chains of guilt, provide you lasting peace, and be at your side as you walk in the freedom of divine mercy. He will pick you up when you stumble and welcome you back into his presence.

Place your trust in him today. He loves you and wants to give you a fresh start.

Amen.

Things for which Christ has forgiven me:

1. _____
2. _____
3. _____
4. _____
5. _____
6. _____
7. _____
8. _____
9. _____
10. _____

Though your sins are like scarlet, they shall be as white as snow.
— Isaiah 1:18 —

Things for which I must forgive others:

1. _____

2. _____

3. _____

4. _____

5. _____

6. _____

7. _____

8. _____

9. _____

10. _____

For if you forgive other people when they sin against you, your heavenly Father will also forgive you.
— Matthew 6:14 —

Ways I can be an ambassador of grace:

1. _____
2. _____
3. _____
4. _____
5. _____
6. _____
7. _____
8. _____
9. _____
10. _____

Live a life worthy of the calling you have received.
— Ephesians 4:1 —

www.ingramcontent.com/pod-product-compliance
Lightning Source LLC
Chambersburg PA
CBHW051841090426
42736CB00011B/1910